4/95

Following the Pack

The World of Wolf Research

Mike Link and Kate Crowley

Voyageur Press

Photographs copyright as follows:
  Photo © by Diane Boyd: page 49.
  Photos © by Fred Harrington: page 52 bottom left; page 162 bottom right; page
    163; page 166 right inset; page 168 bottom left; page 168 bottom right.
  Photos © by Karen Hollett: page 50 middle inset; pages 50–51.
  Photo © by John & Karen Hollingsworth: page 161 inset.
  Photos © by John and Ann Mahan: page 50 top inset; page 52 top; page 53.
  Photos © by Christopher May: page 54 top inset; page 56; page 162 top; page
    162 bottom left; page 166 left inset.
  Photos © by Rick McIntyre: page 54 bottom inset; pages 54–55; pages 164–165.
  Photos © by L. David Mech: page 50 bottom inset; page 52 bottom right; page 56
    inset.
  Photo © by J. H. Robinson: page 161.
  Photos © by Richard Smith: page 165 left inset; page 165 right inset.
  Photos © by Scot Stewart: pages 166–167; page 168 top.

Text editing, design, and layout by Jane McHughen Publishing Services
Cover designed by Leslie Dimond

Printed in Canada
94   95   96   97   98   5   4   3   2   1

Library of Congress Cataloging-in-Publication Data
Link, Michael.
        Following the pack : the world of wolf research / by Mike Link and
Kate Crowley.
        p.   cm.
        Includes index.
        ISBN 0-89658-199-3
        1. Wolves—Research. 2. Wolves. 3. Mammalogists. I. Crowley, Kate.
II. Title. III. Title: Wolf researchers.
        QL737.C22L5   1994
        599.74'442—dc20   93–21358
                                     CIP

Published by **Voyageur Press, Inc.**
P.O. Box 338, 123 North Second Street, Stillwater, MN 55082 U.S.A.
From Minnesota and Canada 612-430-2210 • Toll-free 800-888-9653

Voyageur Press books are also available at discounts for quantities for educational,
fundraising, premium, or sales-promotion use. For details, contact our marketing
department. Please write or call for our free catalog of natural history publications.

Dedication

To the memory of Matthew Link
In life an inspiration,
In death still a companion
May 28, 1968–December 17, 1989

Contents

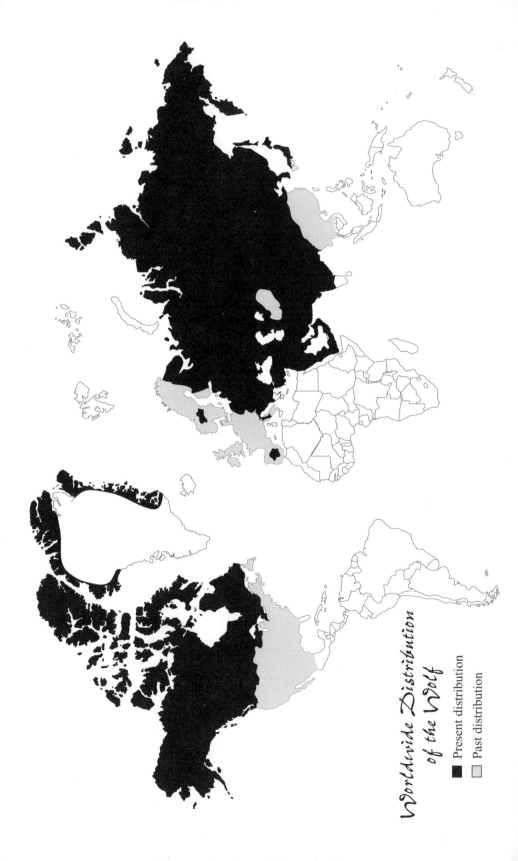

Worldwide Distribution
of the Wolf

■ Present distribution

▨ Past distribution

Preface

THIS BOOK IS A look at many of the people who have worked to get close to the wolf. The researchers we interviewed over the course of the past five years are people who have wandered in wolf country and have taken the time to observe, record, and interpret wolf behavior. Through their eyes, we delve into the wolves' world and examine the interaction between wolf biology and national politics and cultures.

In choosing the wolf researchers for this book, we looked to the IUCN Wolf Specialist Group as it existed when the project began. Based on interviews with all members, we then chose those individuals with the most interesting and most complete stories. Lack of information and detail precluded the inclusion of Dr. Gao from China and Dr. Bibikov from Russia. If individuals were more administrative than field oriented, we looked for a more field-oriented individual. This was the reason for choosing Mike Phillips for the red wolf, even though Warren Parker was the official in charge of the Red Wolf Project.

The world of wolf research is ongoing and constantly evolving. We've included Diane Boyd because she is the only woman with a long-term involvement in wolf field studies; she has gained a strong and positive reputation within the field, and she has a fascinating story to tell. Erik Isaksen is colorful and will never be a bureaucratic wildlife manager, but he has established a reputation and has a long-term commitment that affords him the opportunity to voice strong opinions as a field technician.

Around the globe, there are numerous individuals who have worked, and continue to work, on field projects. They are too numerous to mention, and their work is often short term and degree-driven.

People like Mike Fairchild, Steve Fritts, Mike Nelson, Adrian Wydeven, Dick Thiel, Tom Meier, John Burch, and Layne Adams have worked in Montana, Minnesota, Wisconsin, and Alaska and represent part of the army of individuals who have added to our collective knowledge of the wolf. They, like their counterparts throughout the world, add to a base from which those individuals selected in this book learn, make decisions, and continue their research.

Of primary importance is Durward L. Allen, the Purdue University professor who initiated the most famous wolf study ever done: the Isle Royale wolf-moose investigation. Not only has this study yielded invaluable insights into wolf ecology, but it also produced some of the biologists we feature: L. David Mech and Rolf Peterson, who began as Allen's graduate students.

Like the wolves that are being studied, the individuals in this book are but a sample of the overall population of researchers. It is our hope that we have chosen most of the Alphas in the tales we tell.

Through the stories of these researchers you will learn more about the wolf and the challenge of its survival; however, just as there are no limits to the questions we need to ask about the wolf, there are also no easy answers to the dilemma of human-wolf existence. This book will give you an insight into different perspectives about wolf management programs. It offers much to think about but presents no single conclusion for the future of this fascinating animal. That is a question that will exercise researchers and politicians for as long as wolves continue to share their range with humans.

Wolf of Legend, Wolf of Fact

OUR ATTITUDES TOWARD wolves are shaped by history, folklore, and culture, and responses to wolves vary enormously around the world. In the Ojibwa culture of Mike's great-great grandmother, all animals are endowed with a unique and singular power. For the wolf, it is fidelity. The wolf totem (*mah-een-gun*) is part of the warrior band and represents perseverance and guardianship. In the ceremonial practices of the Midewewin, medicine pouches may be made of wolf skin. In their creation story, one of the four most important spirits in the Ojibwa religion, Nanabojo (also Winebozo, Nanabush, Wenebojo, and other variations), is befriended and cared for by his "nephew" wolf. The wolves in the story demonstrate pack behavior observed by the Indians: They curl up near each other to share warmth, regurgitate food from the hunt to share with family members, and remain faithful at all times. In this and other Ojibwa tales, the wolf is revered for its positive influence and high family values.

In Ojibwa tales, the wolf is revered for its positive influence and high family values

Many Native American groups, especially those whose economy was based primarily on hunting, respected the wolf. The Oneida or Wolf Clan in Wisconsin observed its ability as a hunter: the way it moved stealthily and silently through the landscape; its devotion to family life and the pack; its stoicism, bravery, and endurance. These were qualities that the Native American hunter emulated and encouraged in himself and others.

In most documented Lakota stories, the wolf is good. In only one interview by James Walker, a physician on Pine Ridge Reservation from 1896 to 1914, was the wolf isolated as an evil spirit that would not go to the spirit world. In most stories, wolves teach people. One man related that wolf dreamers always went to their enemies' tipis like a wolf (inconspicuously). They also knew where bison were from their dreams. Wolves are such powerful animal spirits that a gun used to shoot a wolf will not work the next time, and a horse used to chase a wolf will go lame.

The Nunamiut Eskimos of Alaska still speak of wolves as hunters like themselves. In the Inuit tales, nothing is harmful in the order of nature. Predators and prey regulate each other's populations, which is a wisdom that man has not attained.

In the Inuit tale of the Gift of Kaila (deity of the sky), the beginning of the world has only one man and woman. They were alone with no fish in the water, no birds in the sky, and no other creatures to share the earth. The woman's curiosity could not find enough to occupy it because her eyes would always meet an empty sky and her steps did not cross the path of anyone else. One day she dug a hole in the ice bank and she began to fish. One after the other she pulled all the animals from the hole. The caribou came last.

Kaila announced that the caribou was his gift, the most beautiful that he could offer: The caribou would nourish the Inuit people. The woman liberated the animal, ordering him to populate the land and to multiply, and the son of the woman soon could hunt for his livelihood. One day, only the small, skinny, and sick caribou remained. Kaila listened to the complaints of the woman and then asked Amarok, the spirit of the wolf, to place his children on the trail of the small, thin, and sick caribou so that the caribou could once again become big and fat. This is why the caribou and the wolf are one.

In contrast to these benign views of the wolf, we know that the Navajo feared wolves because they believed they might have been human witches. Indeed, the Navajo word for wolf, *mai-coh,* is a synonym for witch. A Navajo witch became a werewolf by wearing a wolf skin, and usually took this shape to kill someone. The Navajo belief resembles European legends about werewolves, and the fear of the Navajo is akin to the traditional fear of nearly all people in the Old World.

The wolf was not always an evil character in the Old World, but over time the traditional tales changed. We can find our best example of this shift of position in the stories of Italy. The founding of the city of Rome and the Roman culture depended on the family values of the wolf. In a family squabble, the rule of the region we now know as Italy was in question. While an evil brother sought to overwhelm his sibling, he sent a servant to eliminate his great nephews—Romulus and Remus. The servant could not destroy the children, but left them in the woods. A female wolf adopted them and raised them (this was a precursor of Kipling's *Jungle Book*). The story evolves with more human competition, and in the end only the wolf does not engage in murder or intrigue. Later in Italian literature, however, Dante makes the wolf a symbol for greed in his epic description of Hell.

Changes in European attitude may have come about partly because in the fourteenth century Europe experienced times of massive deaths from disease, war, and famine. Each event exceeded the capacity of the living to handle the dying. Bodies piled up outside communities; corpses rotted and attracted scavengers, who were found eating human flesh. People felt revulsion and horror at the devouring of their dead. Perhaps the sight of wolves leaving a pile of bodies during the full moon, when the nightmare scene was especially visible, not only made people fear and despise wolf the animal, but also gave shape to a nocturnal terror—werewolves. No doubt these grizzly sights powerfully affected the human psyche, as did real and imagined wolf predation on livestock.

Stories of wolves attacking living humans thrive in the Old World. These stories defy our knowledge of the animals and their behavior in the United States, where we have only one documented record of a wolf attacking a human, and that was a rabid wolf in the 1800s. Because of the prevalence of wolf attacks on humans in Russian literature and art, there are some researchers who wonder if Russian wolves might have behaved differently from North American wolves. In the Middle East, where rabies is a continual problem, there is some belief that the disease, which will affect canines, is the root of the mythology.

We know little about the Middle East and the Eastern wolf tales, but we do know that despite the harmonious natural philosophy of the Eastern regions, the wolf was eliminated throughout major geographic areas. Even today, wolf researchers in India, China, and other locations must try to sort out the truth in stories about wolf killings.

In India, a leopard expert feels that the wolf is blamed for leopard predation on small children. In China, two men present a tale of a recent kill that is flimsy at best, yet their sincerity speaks of the lack of knowledge that their country has about the wolf. In the book *Wolves of the World,* Paul Joslin concludes his essay on Iranian wolves with the following account, which typifies the circumstantial evidence that surrounds the term "wolf attack."

> I followed up on the only report of a shepherd having been attacked and supposedly killed by wolves. Eventually, I located a shepherd who had witnessed the man's death. Both had been attending a flock of sheep when about a dozen wolves appeared. One shepherd worked at bunching the flock while the other, with the aid of three dogs, attempted to drive off the wolves. The dogs pulled down one wolf and the shepherd clubbed it to death with his cane. Meanwhile, a boy who also witnessed the attack ran for help. Several men from the local village arrived and helped drive the remaining wolves off. At this point, the shepherd with the dogs sat down, coughed, and died. The cause of his death was unknown, but it certainly was not a wolf kill.

For the ancient Egyptians, as night like day was necessary, so too was death inevitable. The wolf was associated with birth and destruction and was a conductor of souls across the night of the tomb until the rebirth of the Sun. The Egyptians believed that after a pharaoh died, his ship carried him for a last trip to meet the Sun. Strange gods presided at the ceremony, where the future of the deceased was decided. Each shadow was an obstacle on the way to the Sun, and at each intersection the soul might get lost. To serve as their guide on these dangerous routes, the Egyptians invoked Oupouaout, the god with the head of the wolf — he who "opens the paths" — for he had the privilege of watching over the Sun in his nightly journey.

In the Bible, Isaiah, the most nature-oriented of all the Old and New Testament Scriptures, has two nearly identical references to the wolf. As the author describes the concept of heaven, he envisions wolves lying down with lions in a realm where the predators become grazers and pacifists. An interesting concept, and one that is hard to picture. Note, though, that although the author doesn't like predation, at least he does not advocate the elimination of wolves.

Despite the widespread European fear of wolves, the power of the wolf did surface from time to time in ways other than the fear, hatred, and protective prayers of the people. Charles Estienne Liebault published a collection of French folk beliefs in 1680. Those describing wolf medicines remind us of what was left of a different, perhaps older, connection between European people and wolves: "A wolf's tooth worn by a child protects it from night fears," and, "Wolf-skin shoes make children strong and brave." Pieces of this earlier relationship can be seen in European names. The Irish surname O'Connor with all its variations is derived from Conchobhar, the Gaelic word for "wolf-lover." It is an historic name in at least five districts of Ireland. In Germany, Wulf and variations of it are common surnames.

The constellation Lupus, the Wolf, is not commonly known today, but it was listed in Alfonsine's Tables around 1200 A.D. Located partly in the Milky Way, this constellation lies south of Libra and Scorpio. In the same star group are the Panther, the beast of death, and the Lioness. In another version, Lupus was known as Martius, with the wolf being sacred to Mars, the god of war. It is unclear what the symbolism is, but it does attest to the fact that the wolf was a part of the culture and mythology of the pre–1200 world.

Ancient traditions celebrating the wolf continue in some parts of the world today. In the Caucasus Mountains in southwestern Russia, the people celebrate the festival of Igby at the end of January, just as the United States celebrates Ground Hog Day. The villagers maintained their celebration even though the Communists banned such activities. The celebration marks the end of winter and the primary characters in this pageant are the bots (magical wolves), who go from house to house exacting tribute. There are other elements to this elaborate rite of winter passage, but for our purpose the important element is how the wolves are portrayed by the celebrants. The wolf is portrayed negatively as a representation of intimidation and greed, but it is also playful and magical—both positive attributes.

The American colonists embraced the prevailing European hatred for the wolf rather than the Native Americans' understanding of their

> *Ancient traditions celebrating the wolf continue in some parts of the world today*

character. By the time the United States was being colonized in the seventeenth century, Europe had already declared war on the wolf. The impact of this action would mean the extirpation of wild wolves from over half of their North American range. Where they once roamed all over the continent, wolves were now reduced to ranges in Canada, Alaska, and northeastern Minnesota. In 1624, an English inspection team reported from Plymouth Plantation, "The country is annoyed with foxes, and wolves." The settlers responded, "So are many other good countries, too, but poyson, traps and other such means will help to destroy them."

In 1630, Massachusetts Bay Colony passed this law: "Euy Englishe man that killeth a wolfe in any pte within the limits of this pattent shall have allowed him ld [penny] for euy beast & horse & ob. for every weaned swyine & goate in euy plantacon, to be levied by the constables of sd plantacons." The book *The Standard Library of Natural History,* published in 1901–02, described the wolf as follows: "This great enemy of man and his dependents, the creature against the ravages of which almost all the early races of Europe had to combine either in tribes, villages, or principalities to protect their children."

As the following passage from Samuel Hearne's *A Journey from Prince of Wales Fort in Hudson's Bay to the Northern Ocean* (1769) indicates, Indian respect was not the same as worship, and even in societies where wolf killing was not advocated, it was tolerated. "It is true, some of them will reprimand their youth for talking disrespectfully of particular beasts and birds; but it is done with so little energy, as to be often retorted back in derision. Neither is this, nor their custom of not killing wolves and quiquehatches [wolverines, predators of the beaver] universally observed, and those who do it can only be viewed with more pity and contempt than the others; for I always found it arose merely from the greater degree of confidence which they had in the supernatural power of the conjurers, which induced them to believe, that talking lightly or disrespectfully of anything they seemed to approve, would materially affect their health and happiness in this world."

When the Europeans came to North America they brought diseases that decimated the American Indian. In addition, in the notes of David Thompson and other significant explorers and traders, there are accounts of unusual wildlife deaths. Thompson wrote, "With the death of the Indians . . . the numerous herds of bison and deer also disappeared both in the woods and in the plains, and the Indians about Cumberland House declared the same of the moose, and the swan." According to Thompson, the Indians who were dying of smallpox said, "The Great Spirit having brought this calamity on them, had also taken away the animals in the same proportion." He added, "All the wolves and dogs that fed on the bodies of these that died of smallpox lost their hair especially on the sides and belly, and even for six years wolves were found in this condition and their furr [sic] useless." In the Micmac nation and in other eastern tribes, the animal spirits were blamed for the diseases that affected humans and a war was declared on the beaver.

The lure of trade goods, and the confusion created by rampant disease and Jesuit missionary zeal that accompanied each fur company, overturned the system that was in place and created an un-paralleled wildlife consumerism that created havoc on the North American continent. The situation was particularly bad for the wolf. In addition to the fur trader/trapper's desire for wolf skins was his desire to eliminate a competitor.

In the world today, wolves exist in large numbers only in northern North America, China, and parts of the former Soviet Union. Small populations can be found in Scandinavia, Eastern Europe, Spain, Portugal, Italy, and Greece. The subject of wolves elicits the widest range of emotions of any animal. More people hear about the reintroduction to Yellowstone and the arguments over wolf management in Minnesota and Alaska than most other wildlife issues.

The difficult task is separating the wolf of legend from the wolf of fact

The wolf is an animal of mythology and a complex member of our biological community. The difficult task is separating the wolf of legend from the wolf of fact, and the difficulty lies not just with those who hate the wolf, but also with those who have created a romantic image of the animal and support it with such fervor that they refuse to acknowledge its natural role in ecology.

Understanding the wolf and protecting its place in the environment doesn't happen by saying that the wolf eats only mice. Nor does it happen by trying to make the wolf into a house pet. We can't ignore the anguish of pet owners who have lost their dogs to wolves, or of livestock owners who have suffered economic losses in their herds. In the long run, our efforts to maintain the wolf as a viable part of our ecological world will be based on the accuracy of our information. The information is the product of years and years of research, added to generations of observation and refined through questions, testing hypotheses, and layers of data. The information gathered by researchers must debate and replace the misconceptions and fears of our various cultures.

Fortunately, wildlife has gained an international respect, and despite those who still cling to a "What good is it?" attitude, the prevalent philosophy is one of harmony and sharing the earth. To accomplish this we must understand the organisms that live with us. We need to know their life requirements for space, water, air, and habitat. Once the philosophical questions are resolved, we need biological and ecological data to guide our decisions.

The story of the wolf and wolf research is also the story of our growing knowledge of the earth and its complexity

As far as we know, only human society is more complex than that of wolves. We've studied our own species informally for thousands of years and formally for at least two hundred. With all that data, who would dare to say that we understand ourselves? We shall always be observers and participants in life. There will never be too much knowledge. The story of the wolf and wolf research is also the story of our growing knowledge of the earth and its complexity. Perhaps the study of the wolf will eventually lead to a better understanding of ourselves.

1

Early Researchers

TO GO BEYOND the anthropological and social symbolism of wolves we must rely on the fieldwork of the researcher, for it is the researcher who confronts the questions in the minds and on the lips of the public, and who tries to sort out, in a systematic way, the factors that induce the wolf to behave as it does.

Sigurd Olson

It was over sixty years ago that Minnesota naturalist Sigurd Olson, former president of the U.S. Wilderness Society, author of numerous canoe country books, and spokesman for the Boundary Waters Canoe Area Wilderness, conducted the first systematic research on the wolf.

The report that resulted was called "The Size and Organization of the Pack" and was published in *Scientific Monthly* in 1938. When Sig began his thesis study, the major work on wolves was a book on mammals of North America by Thomas Ernest Seton. This book was popular, but differed from Seton's normal popular writing in that he collected the available knowledge on each of the species and attempted to present a scientifically accurate book for the general public. Sig found this book at the beginning of his research project in 1930. When he read it he was crestfallen. He wrote to his professor in Illinois and asked what was left to learn. In one of the classic advisor/student letters of all time, Professor Kahn detailed the questions Sig should ask himself:

Find out all you can about the animals in your region. Never mind Manitoba or Newfoundland, or Labrador. Check him on every point you can. Support him where you can with new evidence. Contradict him at every point you can with new evidence. Remember that no one's work stands alone. . . . Remember that no one knows all there is to know about any one animal. Try to make your knowledge of the form as complete as possible. Try to go beyond surfaces. Try to analyze why your wolf is doing what he is doing. What the factors are that determine the actions, or reactions. What does he eat? What does he reject as food? Why does he not eat other things? Look at him as a reaction to the actions around him, then look at him as an action causing reaction around him. . . . He is not a thing apart. Life is made up of actions, reactions, and interactions. Think Sig, what that little sentence means. Turn it around and look at it carefully. It opens a new horizon and paints a different colored picture. Take your wolf from that point of view if you wish. No one has attempted it in any mammal before. Think it over.

Sig collected data accumulated by wolf trappers. He sorted through the speculation and inaccuracies of wolf lore, recording specific observations that would lead to an understanding of wolf packs, their ranges, and their role as part of the ecology of the north country. Although later research improved on many aspects of Sig's initial research, some of his conclusions were confirmed forty years later by radio tracking.

In a short note entitled "The Organization and Range of the Pack" published in *Ecology* magazine in January of 1938 (and part of the 1938 *Scientific Monthly* article), Sig wrote, "Packs vary in number from 5–30, the smaller group being by far the most common." He also observed, "Wolves sometimes kill big game while hunting alone, but most of the actual killing is done either by the members of the last season's family, or in the case of a large pack, by several packs which have banded together." He noted, "Ordinarily they have a beat which they cover every two or three weeks, and a trapper who knows the route of a pack can bank on the possibility of its appearance in a certain locality regularly. . . . The course a pack travels is in the shape of a great, uneven circle, the diameter of which is often thirty to fifty miles [48–80 km]. The extent of the run depends on the supply of game. If game is plentiful the circle may be small. If scarce, it may be several hundred miles in length. The fact that hunting is always easier in the region which has been undisturbed for several weeks may account, at least partly, for the great range of some of the hunting trails."

Sig was a biology instructor in Ely Junior College in northeastern Minnesota at the time of this research. He applied his knowledge as a biology instructor together with his professional guide experience and gave us the platform from which future wolf research around the world could grow. This knowledge would be shared with his students and the devotees of his books, who would lead the charge for understanding and protection of the wolf from the 1950s through to the present.

Aldo Leopold

While science was advancing, so was environmental philosophy. Aldo Leopold had been a leader in the campaign by sportsmen and stockmen to eradicate wolves, mountain lions, and other large predators from the deer and cattle ranges of Arizona and New Mexico. He told delegates at a National Game Conference in New York in 1920, "It's going to take a lot of patience and money to catch the wolf or lion in New Mexico, but the last one must be caught before the job can be fully successful."

In 1944, Leopold had an experience that would change the way he thought about predators. In an essay called "Thinking Like a Mountain" he wrote,

We reached the old wolf in time to watch a fierce green fire dying in her eyes. I realized then and have known ever since that there was something new to me in those eyes, something known only to her and to the mountain. I was young then, and full of trigger itch. I thought that less wolves would mean more deer, and no wolves would mean hunters' paradise. But after seeing the green fire die, I sensed that neither the wolf nor the mountain would agree with such a view.

He also wrote,

Since then, I have lived to see state after state extirpate its wolves. I have watched the face of many a newly wolf-less mountain and seen the south facing slopes wrinkle with a maze of new deer trails. I have seen every edible bush and seedling browsed, first to anemic desuetude, and then to death. I have seen every edible tree defoliated to the height of a saddle horn. Such a mountain looks as if someone had given God new pruning shears, and forbidden Him all other exercise. In the end the starved bones of the hoped-for deer herd, dead of its own too much, bleached with the bones of dead sage, or moulder under the high line junipers.

Leopold discovered that a buck taken by wolves could be replaced in two or three years, but a range of plants browsed by an overpopulation of deer may never replace itself. This discovery was one of the major advances in the study and science of ecology, and Leopold was on the leading edge of this new movement. In 1939, he presented a paper to the Society of American Foresters and the Ecological Society entitled "A Biotic View of Land." In this paper he presented an image of the land as a biotic pyramid, a fountain of energy flowing through a circuit of soil, plants, and animals. The whole track of evolution, he suggested, was to elaborate and diversify the biotic repertoire, adding layer upon layer to the pyramid and link after link to the food chains of which it was composed.

In presenting these views, Leopold was creating the science of game management. A proper function of management, to him, was to encourage the greatest possible diversity in an attempt to preserve the widest possible realm in which natural processes might seek their equilibrium. He made it clear that the wolf was one of the large carnivores that belonged at the very apex of the biotic pyramid. Eventually the wolf would become Leopold's symbol of land health.

In "Thinking Like a Mountain," Leopold put his ideas into a text that the general public could understand. In his 1933 textbook, *Game Management,* he explained the science of management and gave depth to his understanding of predation. In the chapter entitled "Predator Control" he says, "Predator control has received more attention than any other factor except hunting. . . . Unfortunately, much of this attention and many predator control operations have been based upon assumed or traditional predator/game relationships or at best on generalizations supported only by a small number of observations which were, in the light of present knowledge, often misinterpreted." It is clear more data was needed.

Adolph Murie

In 1939, Adolph Murie began the first major wolf research project in the world that concentrated on the collection of field data. One of the results of this work was the publication of the book entitled *The Wolves of Mount McKinley.* In his introduction, Murie writes,

In 1939, I was requested to make a study of relationships between the timber wolf and the Dall sheep in Mount McKinley [Denali] National Park, Alaska. I arrived in the Park on April 14, and three days later was taken twenty-two miles [35 km] into the Park by dogteam and left at a cabin on Sanctuary River, where I started my field work. The next morning I climbed a mountain and saw a ewe and yearling on the grass slope. The first white sheep I had seen for sixteen years. A little later through the field glasses, I picked up a beautiful ram resting on a ledge, the graceful curved horns silhouetted against the spring blue sky. A strong cold wind was blowing on top, so I slipped on my parka. During the day, sixty-six sheep were classified, twenty of which were yearlings. Wolf tracks were seen and wolf droppings containing sheep hair was [sic] found. The long, slow process of gathering data had begun.

Like Sig Olson, Adolph worked in the wilderness. He worked without a data base, so he needed to collect all the observations he could before conclusions could be attempted. In his book, Adolph adds this observation, "The strongest impression remaining with me, after watching the wolves on numerous occasions, was their friendliness. The adults were friendly towards each other, and were amiable towards the pups, at least as late as October. This good feeling has been strongly marked in three captive wolves which I have known." As if to test this amiability, Murie approached a den. When he was twelve feet (3.6 m) away, the female darted out. Adolph continued on to the den, crawling in and removing a pup. He noted that the male and female did nothing but bark.

The study was triggered by the U.S. National Park Administration's uncertainty about its own policy toward wolves. Murie formulated the following questions for his research: What is the total effect of wolf preying on the big-game species in this national park? What is the relationship between the wolves of the park and the general wolf population of Alaska? How do predators affect hoofed animals? In short, What is the ecological picture centering on the wolf of Mount McKinley National Park?

Murie's study ran from April 1939 to August 1941. He had an assistant in 1939, but worked alone in both 1940 and 1941. The results were published in 1944. He included notes on caribou, moose, grizzly bear, fox, and eagle. He calculated that in 1939 he walked approximately 1,700 miles (2,720 km) doing his research. During the winter he traveled on skis and dogsled.

Murie's research brought this important insight. "It appears that wolves depended mainly on weak classes of sheep. That is the old, the diseased, and the young in their first year. Such predation would seem to benefit the species over a long period of time. It indicates a normal predator/prey adjustment in Mount McKinley National Park. These conclusions are based on the study of 829 sheep remains, mainly skulls gathered on the range."

Milt Stenlund

The next major wolf researcher on the scene was Milt Stenlund from Ely, Minnesota. In 1940, Sigurd Olson, then dean of the Ely Junior College, advised Milt to consider entering the new field of fish and wildlife management at the University of Minnesota. After time at the university and in the military, Milt returned to the canoe country and the wolves for his master's program. As both a master's candidate and an employee of the Minnesota Conservation Department (later renamed the Department of Natural Resources), Milt was based in

Ely as the area game biologist. For the next five years he would work in the field on the greatest and most enjoyable chapter of his career and life.

By this time, the wolf had already been eliminated from 85 percent of its former U.S. range and had viable populations in only Alaska and northeastern Minnesota. Milt describes one of the experiences that led to his fascination with wolves. "A pack of wolves slowly and silently walked down the lake in a single file, their heads like gray beads on a leather thong. The lead wolf passed in front of me. He looked briefly in my direction, but paid no attention to me or the campsite on the shore. Now the second and third animals passed in silence with the descending darkness and the falling snow. It seemed almost unreal. Now the pack had passed and was traveling swiftly down the far shore. They again grouped momentarily near the point and then dispersed into the snow covered spruce. They had come and gone in a complete silence, leaving only a neat trail which was already filling with new snow."

Milt's original proposal, known as Big Game Job #63, was entitled "An Ecological Study of the Wolf/Deer Relationship in Minnesota." The purpose was to research food habits of the wolves by collecting and examining stomach contents. Personnel in the field kept notes on wolf activities and investigated reported deer kills to determine the cause of death. All this information was to be evaluated to document the importance of the wolf as a predator on deer, and to document the distribution, movement, and number of wolves in the area.

A pack of wolves slowly and silently walked down the lake in a single file, their heads like gray beads on a leather thong

Sig Olson had estimated one wolf per ten square miles (one wolf per 26 km²). The working estimate for Milt's project was one wolf per seventeen square miles (one wolf per 44.2 km²). Without the help of radio collars or other modern tracking techniques, Milt had to use the most reliable data available, but it still amounted to an educated guess. Later work by L. David Mech confirmed that both estimates could have been correct.

Milt's was an exceedingly ambitious undertaking, and he soon learned that winter with its tracks and lack of leaves on the trees was the best time for his research. He stored wolf carcasses in his garage or in the airplane hangar in Winton, northeast of Ely. When the carcasses began to thaw in the spring, his work picked up to a furious pace because the smell upset the neighbors—and probably the other researchers too. He recalls in his book, *Popple Leaves and Boot Oil,* "Several times I completely lost my appetite and went without eating." Deer were found in 80 percent of the wolves' stomachs and made up 96 percent of the volume of food. Snowshoe hare, porcupine, ruffed grouse, and unidentified animals made up the remaining 4 percent.

Milt's career as a scientist with the Conservation Department put him in the public arena. On the basis of Milt's master's thesis, his supervisor, Richard Dorer, determined in 1958 that wolf control by game personnel would cease in the wilderness areas of the Superior National Forest. This was a monumental step towards wolf preservation in Minnesota. The wolves also benefited from the 1949 ban on airplanes flying lower than four thousand feet (1,200 m) above sea level over the wilderness.

Durward L. Allen

In 1949, the first wolf tracks were found on Isle Royale National Park, a forty-five-mile- (72-km-) long island in Lake Superior. The park was created in 1940. It was then, and remains today, a wilderness without roads, hunting, or permanent settlement. It has also been declared an International Biosphere Preserve.

When the wolves crossed over the ice from Canada in 1949, the park was home to as many as three thousand moose. It was a perfect laboratory, one that represented an ecological zone where natural interactions between wolves and moose could be studied with minimum interference from humans. In 1958, Durward L. Allen of Purdue University decided to take advantage of this unusual situation and initiated a study that continues to the present.

Beginning in June of 1958, L. David Mech, a graduate student of Allen's, began a three-year study to explore the dynamics of the moose and wolf relationship on Isle Royale. At this time, there was also a great deal of activity in Canada. Ian Cowan published a report in British Columbia in 1955. In 1958, Doug Pimlott began a study of the wolves of Algonquin Park, in Ontario. Pimlott became known as the father of wolf research in Canada, and became one of the country's most respected scientists. David Mech, through his work in northern Minnesota, would become the father of wolf research in the United States and then go on to become the world's foremost authority on wolves.

The emphasis on wolf research in the United States switched to Superior National Forest, where Mech began working as a part-time researcher. In 1966, Mech and Dan Frenzel began a study of wolves in the Superior National Forest. Mech's publication on Isle Royale came out in 1966, the same year the Endangered Species Act was passed.

In 1969, Mech was hired by the U.S. Fish and Wildlife Service to establish a Minnesota wolf research program. In 1970, he published his classic book, *The Wolf.* He was then a full-time researcher in Superior National Forest.

Research at this time shifted from incidental observations to active trapping and radio-telemetry. Advances in technology meant that questions that formerly had no opportunity to be answered—and therefore were not asked—could now be formulated and pursued. For the first time, individual wolves could be followed throughout their territory, even when aerial observation was not possible—one lone wolf was found to wander over 350 miles (560 km) from its point of origin. That type of information could now be plotted. It was easier to find wolf dens, and it was easier to see wolf movement in all seasons. Even with advancing technology, however, there still was a great deal to learn. In one attempt to transplant four wolves in the Upper Peninsula of Michigan, the project failed because human attitudes had not been considered thoroughly enough. The education of the local people had not prepared them for acceptance of wolves within their area, and all four wolves were gone within a few months.

Vic Van Ballenberghe

While not all wolf researchers became figures on the level of Sigurd Olson, Aldo Leopold, Adolf Murie, and Milt Stenlund, others contributed relatively early on to the body of knowledge about wolves. In 1975 Vic Van Ballenberghe published a Lake Superior Shoreline study looking at the wolves in relationship to the wintering deer yards. The deer in northern Minnesota find it difficult to survive in the boreal forest complex of the Superior National Forest during the winter. Snow depth limits movement and browse, and the deer have an instinctive migratory pattern that brings them to Lake Superior's shores. Here the angles of the slope collect sunlight, which melts and minimizes the snow cover. An abundance of deer is concentrated within a two- to three-mile (3.2–4.8 km) corridor, which also attracts wolves. At one point in the 1950s, following massive logging, the regenerated forest maintained a population of 525 deer per square mile (210 deer per km^2), but this number could not be sustained. As both the forest and the North Shore's popularity grew, wolves needed to adjust to more humans and less food.

The wolf continually faces new human and biological challenges. The question that we must now confront, the question that periodically comes up when budgets are examined, when individuals are looking for targets for their wrath and frustrations, is, When have we studied enough? When should we stop? Sigurd Olson thought we knew everything in 1930 before his research process even began. In the 1970s, the wolf research on Isle Royale in Lake Superior was nearly wrapped up. Then in 1980–81, the wolf population crashed, and we didn't know enough to answer the question, Why? In Europe, the greatest wolf populations are in the former eastern bloc countries. Can the wolf survive capitalism, private land ownership, and the spread of private guns? Economy and ecology are not always an easy mix. In Saudi Arabia and Iraq, have the thirty-five-pound (16-kg) desert wolves survived Desert Storm? What are the impacts of chemical warfare, burning oil fields, and land mines on the desert mammals? What will the next war do to the wildlife population?

2

L. David Mech: The Wolfman

SINCE THE FIFTIES, the name L. David Mech has become synonymous with wolf research the world over. It is not a case of one man doing all the research, but rather of the world building its research on the models Dave has developed during a lifetime of study.

It would be easy to fill this entire book with information about Dave's studies and what he has learned about the wolf over the last thirty-odd years. He has already written five books and over two hundred articles for scientific journals and popular magazines. While we are fascinated by the animal he studies and constantly crave more knowledge of it, we are also fascinated by the man. What drives a person to spend an entire working lifetime in pursuit of one species? Who is this "Wolfman," and how has he lived all these years as a dedicated scientist?

David Mech is first and foremost a very private person, not given to great expression about his personal life and feelings. He can talk to someone for hours about the wolf and related wildlife studies, but discussion on other social levels does not come so easily. He has publicly admitted that he's uncomfortable around people and doesn't really need them much. This is not to say that he is an unfriendly person. He has a gentle, soft-spoken manner and an easy laugh, but there is always a bit of formality and distance when he is in a social group.

His appearance identifies him as an outdoorsman. He prefers plaid flannel shirts most of the year, and in the winter months a trademark fur hunting cap with earflaps turned up protects his balding head. A brown beard covers a good portion of his face, nearly hiding his mouth. It is obvious from his choice of fashion and the beat-up government vehicle he drives that material wealth is not the most important thing in his life. Wealth of spirit and mind are the things Dave values most. He has a love of classical opera and the theater. His favorite opera is *Mefistofele* by Orrigo Boito. It is not surprising to learn that this opera is about Faust's obsessive quest for knowledge and the devil's bet with God that he can quench it.

Dave Mech's insatiable quest for knowledge about wolves stems from parents who fostered a love of learning and a childhood spent dreaming of wilderness adventure. Born in Syracuse, New York, Dave went fishing and camping with his family and at the age of five received the book *American Wildlife*. Even though he lived in a blue-collar neighborhood of the city, there were ways to escape to wild places. He and like-minded friends caught snakes and salamanders in nearby fields and ponds. Then there was Hunts Hill, a bare knob surrounded by houses, where in the winter he could pretend to be an arctic explorer, as blowing snow hid the surrounding city.

When he was eleven, Dave "exaggerated" his age so that he could join the Boy Scouts and improve his opportunities for outdoor adventure. For a long time he thought he would be an astronomer, since that was the only science he knew existed as a career. Then, when he was fourteen, he attended a conservation camp in the Catskill Mountains. One of the counselors was a wildlife biology major at Cornell University, and suddenly Dave had the direction he had been seeking. Another lifelong interest was sparked at this camp, too. Among the courses offered was one taught by a professional fur trapper. Trapping had no controversy associated with it at the time, and Dave found it to be an excellent way to combine his love of the outdoors with his fascination for mammals. Dave continues to trap today, as his hobby. He says, "There's a phrase known as 'trapping fever,' and any trapper knows what you're talking about. It's an obsession. . . . For me, then and now, the appeal of trapping has little or nothing to do with killing an animal."

Trapping took up all his free time in those teen years. He read everything he could about it and learned that to be successful he had to know a great deal about the animals he was trying to catch. For Dave, it was part of the mystique of trapping. He soon discovered that carnivores were the real challenge. They were wary, and you had to match wits with them. He describes them as "the 'intellectuals' of the furbearers." This, says Dave, "clinched the matter. Someday I would study carnivores."

The money Dave earned through trapping and working in a grocery store thirty hours a week put him through studies at Cornell University that culminated in a degree in wildlife biology. He spent spring and winter vacations with friends in the wilderness of Adirondack State Park, where he gained more firsthand experience observing tracks and sign following otters, beavers, deer, and fishers (a member of the weasel family). In the summer before his senior year Dave got a job on a university research project live trapping, anesthetizing, and handling black bears. This experience solidified his desire to work as a professional scientist in the study of carnivores. Then in 1957, in what seemed like a dream come true, Durward Allen, a professor of wildlife ecology at Purdue University, offered Dave a chance to study wolves on Isle Royale, a completely roadless wilderness. Allen was very impressed with Dave, with his scholarly attitude, and with his experience in the field. He says, "[Dave] was lean and hungry. He had a frugal acceptance of whatever hardships outdoor living might require and a near mystical curiosity about the complexities of nature. He responded with breathless incredulity to what I was offering."

Dave responded with breathless incredulity to what I was offering

On Isle Royale, scientists could study classic predator-prey relationships in a natural laboratory setting. In June of 1958 Dave Mech first set foot on the island. Within a day he saw his first moose and then a large canine footprint on a muddy trail. During that first summer, he hiked hundreds of miles on the trails looking for tracks, sign, and scat. He soon learned that what he was most likely to find were fecal droppings. These were carefully dissected to reveal the diet of the wolves. They yielded mostly moose and, occasionally, beaver hair.

Isle Royale was then a little-known and little-visited national park.

In his four years of study, Dave met only three groups of hikers. The park employees, commercial fishermen, and their families were skeptical about the scientific study and told Dave that there were only six wolves on the island—and that they were eating all the moose. He was also advised to carry a gun to protect himself against the dangerous canines.

Dave took the advice about the gun and has regretted it ever since. During the winter of 1960, he and his bush pilot observed a wolf pack chase and kill a moose. This was Dave's first observation of an actual kill, and he badly wanted to examine the dead animal before it was eaten. The pilot, worried about Dave's safety, urged him not to try, but Dave was determined. They put the plane down on the ice of a nearby lake and agreed on a warning that the pilot would give Dave if it appeared that the wolves were a threat. The pilot took off in the plane, and Dave snowshoed toward the kill site.

Dave had hoped to take movies of the wolves at the kill, but most had run off. When he was about seventy-five feet (22.5 m) away, the two remaining wolves looked up from the moose and ran away. While Dave was standing over the kill examining the internal organs, he heard the plane come roaring toward him, the warning signal he and the pilot had agreed upon. Looking up he saw two wolves rushing through the trees directly at him. "I was twenty-two years old and had a quick decision to make. Should I reach for my movie camera or my revolver? I chose the revolver. Instantly I realized my mistake. Just the movement of my hand was enough to show the wolves that I was a human." From the air, it had looked as though the two wolves had playfully raced one another back to the moose, not realizing Dave was still there. The experience taught Dave that wolves are as afraid of humans as we are of them. He decided that the loaded gun was probably more dangerous than any healthy wolf he'd meet.

In the years since this encounter, Dave has spent countless hours in the presence of wolves, both in the wild and in captive packs, and has learned what they will and will not tolerate from a human. If cornered, frightened, or confused, they will respond automatically with a quick, short bite. Dave has been bitten three times, twice by "tame" wolves and once by a half-drugged wild one, under these circumstances. Over the years, a few reports have come in of wolf attacks on humans in North America, none of them fatal. There is no question in Dave's mind that if the wolves in those attacks had meant to kill the humans, they would have done so. "I have seen wolves attack prey animals, and there is nothing hesitant about the attack. No one could ever grab a wolf by the neck or throat if it lunged the way it does at prey. Wolves can crack open the heavy upper leg bones of musk oxen and sever a cow's tail at the base in a single bite."

Dave's most recent research on the arctic wolves of Ellesmere Island has contributed to his belief in their basic nonaggressive attitude toward humans. These wolves have had little to no contact with people, and Dave was as much of a curiosity to them as they were to him. He has had seven adult wolves surround him as he lay watching their den. He has had a yearling wolf playfully steal his cap after it blew off his head. In one of the most moving experiences of Dave's life, a four-week-old pup toddled up with its mother just a few feet away and tugged on his bootlace, pulling it until it untied. Even after the pack had killed a musk ox and were feeding on it, he was able to crawl on his hands and knees to within twenty feet (6 m) of the wolves without disturbing the alpha pair's meal or being threatened.

Dave's sighting of the moose kill was the beginning of thousands of hours that would be spent observing wolves from the air during the course of his various research projects. Prior to his Isle Royale research, no one had studied wolves in this way, and no one knew if they would tolerate the circling aircraft and behave naturally.

The wolves actually adapted to the aircraft much more quickly than Dave did. This kind of observation meant that the plane had to make numerous tight circles above the animals; for Dave this meant almost constant air sickness. "Each time I spotted a moose, Don Murray dived the plane at it to make it run. Then any other unseen moose nearby also ran and I could count them. This might sound like fun, but just thinking about it makes me airsick," Dave was quoted as saying in his biography, *Wolfman*. Since the plane gave Dave his only real opportunities to observe the wolves and moose, he stuck with it and eventually managed to get his queasy stomach under control (although he still has occasional bouts of air sickness).

Dave's first face-to-face encounter with a wolf came from one of these flights. The pilot put the plane down on the ice just ahead of a pack of wolves. They landed near an old fish house, and Dave and the pilot managed to sneak into it before the wolves showed up. Dave cracked the door open wide enough for a camera lens. One of the wolves came within fifteen feet (4.5 m) and calmly stared at the door and the strange clicking sounds coming from it. "It looked like a big friendly dog," Dave recalls in *Wolfman*. "It was easy to believe that I could have reached out and petted [it]. . . . It certainly helped inspire me to learn all I could about the animal that had such a calm and gentle look, yet earned its living by killing."

Dave's study on Isle Royale ended in 1962 with the completion of his Ph.D. thesis. He returned to the city and to a research associate position at the University of Minnesota. Later he would work as a professor and research ecologist at Macalester College in St. Paul. He had a wife and four children and a home in the suburbs, but his heart was still in the north country. For a period when he was not formally employed, he wrote *The Wolf: Ecology and Behavior of an Endangered Species*. He also began preliminary studies of wolves in northeastern Minnesota.

Then in 1967, he got a call from St. Paul's Como Zoo asking whether he would take and raise two wolf pups. He knew this would not be an easy task either for him or for his young family, but he also believed it would provide him with a unique opportunity to gain knowledge about wolves' early development. The pups were ten days old, a male they named Thunder and a female named Lightning. Dave's children immediately fell in love with the pups, as did the family dog.

Dave thought they were going to have one big happy pack until, at twenty-seven days of age, Thunder and Lightning began fighting. The fighting was in earnest, not playful, and drew blood from Lightning. Dave thought they would have to return one pup to the zoo. Shortly before Lightning's scheduled departure, the two were put on the lawn together. Once again they fought, only this time Lightning rolled onto her back and whined. Thunder raised his tail and the question of dominance was settled. They fought no more. Now they could enjoy one another's company.

Unfortunately, Thunder developed distemper at the age of three and a half months. Lightning became sick too, but survived. At five months, her behavior changed again. She became afraid of strangers and threatened some unfamiliar dogs, although she remained friendly and affectionate with her family and familiar dogs. Lightning swam in a nearby creek with the Mech children and occasionally woke Dave in the mornings by leaping onto the bed. As she grew, so did Dave's concern about her presence in the neighborhood. She was circled by a high fence and kept on a long lead line, but still she managed to escape.

One of the ways Dave has judged wolves' intelligence is by the ways they manage to escape. "You'd never believe they could figure those things out," he says. "Not as pups, but when they get really experienced. We've watched them with drop-doors where the cable goes up and over the roof of the pen and then comes down to a panel outside the pen. It's not even visible really. We've seen a wolf that was very experienced at escaping jump up to a little two-inch [5-cm] gap between the top pipe and the roof and grab that cable enough times that the door would get stuck and out he'd go.

"The captive wolves were motivated to escape because they were being darted regularly and this creates a fear response. When they're scared, it's incredible what they'll do. I had a ceiling about ten feet [3 m] high. I brought a class in one time to see Lightning. She was down the hallway and we were in the living room, and she got so scared of all the people that she jumped from a standing position, just sprang right up, and touched her back on the ceiling."

The experience of raising wolves at home taught Dave a lot about them and about their natural instincts and abilities, but it also taught him that they are not animals to be kept as pets. After Lightning ran away, tasted freedom, and was returned to her home and the chain, he saw her struggle, whine, and pace, seeking freedom again. Empathizing with "his" wolf, Dave realized that it is wrong to try to tame a wolf. Dave says, "They are made for other wolves and for vast expanses of wilderness."

Wolves are made for other wolves and for vast expanses of wilderness

Dave took Lightning back to the zoo she came from and asked them to find a home for her in another zoo where she would have room to run. He couldn't bear to see her in a cage for the rest of her life. He never saw her again, but it is easy to understand the deep emotions he felt for the animal when you read his words in the preface of his book, *The Wolf*. "And lastly, to Lightning—if it is permissible to address a wolf in print. The only thing I can say is, 'I'm sorry.'"

In 1969, Dave began work for the U.S. Fish and Wildlife Service in the same position he holds today as a wildlife research biologist. He had begun to radio collar wolves in northern Minnesota in 1968. That fall and winter five were captured and radio tagged. It was not an easy task, because wolves are so intelligent and naturally wary. By 1970, fifteen wolves were radio collared. Since that time the numbers have fluctuated, with as many as thirty wearing collars at one time.

These radio-collared animals have added a vast amount to our knowledge and understanding of the species. For instance, one wolf traveled almost 500 miles (800 km) in a two-month period; that same animal traveled 122 miles (195 km) in a straight line. The radio collaring was especially useful in discovering more about wolf territories. It has also documented longevity.

One female wolf, #2407, was captured in the fall of 1971 and was estimated to be one and a half years old. She was recaptured and had her radio replaced in the next three years. Then in 1977 her radio failed prematurely, but one of her pups had been collared, and researchers were able to see #2407 from the air and recognize her. Catching #2407 became progressively more difficult as she learned the ways of those seeking to trap her. The last time Dave tried to catch her, he put the traps under water and she pulled them all up.

She was caught again in 1978 and given a special collar with two radios. She wasn't captured again until the summer of 1980 and again in 1982. She was then at least twelve years old, a very old age for a wild wolf. Captive wolves can live to be sixteen years old, but they don't face the constant threats of traps, bullets, and cars speeding down roads. When #2407 was caught in 1980, she had a fox snare around her neck. Somehow she had managed to tear it loose.

Since the project began in 1968, Dave and his assistants have trapped more than five hundred wolves and fitted them with radio collars. This business of trapping wolves is always difficult and very time consuming for the researchers and stressful for the animals. Almost from the beginning, Dave began to imagine an improved method for capture. His dreams became reality in 1987 when he received the patent for his drug-injection capture collars. These have all the features of a radio collar and more. A computer-operated radio transmitter and receiver control two tiny darts that release an anesthetizing drug. All the researchers need to do is to locate the animal and send the signal to bring it down. The collar can also record the level of activity of an animal over a period of time. If it should malfunction, it can be instructed to release from the animal so it can be retrieved for repair or reprogramming.

According to Dave, "Now we can look at wolves more frequently. We can weigh them, test their blood, and learn more about their reproductive capacities if we can easily knock them out for a brief period. You just can't do that if you have to spend most of your time trying to recapture them by trapping."

Some may think that this researcher would have quenched his thirst for knowledge after studying one species for more than thirty years, but for Dave another aspect of his dream has just recently begun and it is one that he feels will continue to hold his interest for the rest of his life: the wolves of Ellesmere Island in the Arctic Circle. "I'll probably return all my life because this is an experience that I just can't top and I don't think I'll ever run out of information to gather," Dave says.

For years he had hoped to spend time living close to and observing a pack, something that is impossible in the thick boreal forests where the majority of wolves live. His dreams were fired by accounts of scientists who had gone to the Arctic and had had close encounters with the wolves that live there.

In 1986, an opportunity arose to go to Ellesmere Island as part of a *National Geographic* magazine assignment, and Dave jumped at the chance. Ellesmere is 1,000 miles (1,600 km) from Alaska, about 1,000 miles (1,600 km) north of the Arctic Circle, and 450 miles (720 km) from the North Pole. It is 300 miles (480 km) north of the nearest Inuit village. There is a government weather station in the area, and the only people who ever come into the region are there for specific purposes. Humans pose no threat to wolves, which may account for the animals' lack of fear.

Spring and summer last four months of the year in the Arctic and are times of total daylight. This is the only time of year researchers can reasonably study the wolves. Even then temperatures remain frigid and the wind blows constantly across the treeless tundra. Two-thirds of the island is permanently covered by ice and snow.

As soon as Dave arrived on Ellesmere he began working with the wolves almost twenty-four hours a day, sharing the hours with photographer Jim Brandenburg. Early on they observed the wolves running up and down a large iceberg in what appeared to be play. Slowly, the two men moved closer to the pack. After ten days, the wolves had become fully acclimated to their presence. The men had become accepted by the pack.

Dave returned to the island in June and set out to find the pack. He was also hoping to locate the den. It took one week. He followed the lactating alpha female, who led him to a rock formation that incorporated a cave. Dave says, "That was the highlight of my life. I mean, I don't see where there would be anything that could come close to that."

After a while, he was allowed to sit near the den, and he even participated in some howling sessions with the pups. But it appears that the wolves felt role reversal was fair play, and the men discovered that the wolves liked to come to their campsite to investigate these two-legged animals.

On one occasion, a wolf stuck his head into the tent door, which was pulled shut with a drawstring. At first, he just stuck his nose in while all the other wolves stood around wagging their tails. Then his head disappeared inside the tent and he pulled it out with Dave's red sleeping bag in his mouth. This reminded Dave of the behavior of wolves when they've made a kill and begin to gut the animal. Fearing that his only bedding would turn into a mass of floating feathers, he let out a sharp hoot. "I didn't want to howl to them, because that might make them think I was a wolf. I don't know what that sound made them think, but they sprang up and took off and ran as fast as they could for about three hundred yards [275 m]. From that time on, they really didn't bother the tent." However, if the men weren't cautious and left things like toilet paper sitting outside the tent, the wolves would grab it and, as Dave says, "strew it all over and decorate the tundra with it."

One of the things Dave was most interested in watching was a hunt. He had seen some moose hunting by wolves from the air, but seeing a hunt close up, on the ground, would be an entirely different experience. When the opportunity arrived, it went beyond his wildest expectations. The wolves set out after a herd of musk oxen. It was a casual confrontation to begin with, but gradually the situation changed with more maneuvering and skirmishes between the wolves and musk ox. As the musk ox ran and swerved around, the wolves grew increasingly excited. In Dave's words, "The scene grew surrealistic; big dark whirling beasts; long white streaks; clouds of dust; swerving, streaking, twisting, charging; black masses, white streaks, dust—the Stone Age!

"Fourteen musk oxen and seven wolves, all in a swirling, chaotic, dusty mass. The noise, the dust, the motion, the frenzy drew us straight into the fray. It grew hard to remain objective. Although I have watched wolf packs chasing moose, deer, and caribou, that was always from an airplane, where I was already a spectator. It was different here. We were almost in the middle of this primeval scene," Dave wrote in *The Arctic Wolf: Living with the Pack.*

When the hunt was completed and the wolves had eaten their fill— and cached what they couldn't eat—they returned to the den, where they slept and socialized. This gave Dave some time to absorb what had taken place. He realized that, "Not only was I actually living with a pack of wolves, but I had just shared an incredibly intense, intimate, and atavistic experience with them. For one who has spent most of his life seeking to know the wolf, this had truly been the ultimate trip."

Dave intends to return to Ellesmere for as long as he's able. Each time he goes there he comes to know the animals as individuals and he admits growing attached to them. Each leave-taking is difficult, knowing that some of the animals may not be there when he returns. Each time he leaves, he prepares himself for another world, which means "shifting my mental gears to help prepare myself to resume my life as a human being."

Asked why people are so fascinated by wolves, he says without hesitation, "The fact that the animal was the progenitor of the dog. Everybody has pet dogs or knows somebody who does, and a wolf is the prototype dog, the original dog. They're beautiful animals. They live in packs and they howl, which gives them some sort of charisma that other animals don't seem to have. They're hunters and have a hard time making a living . . . , there's almost a sexiness to animals that hunt. Compare a raptor with a dove for example, and more people become taken by the raptor."

While we can't know the future of the wolf, we can be sure that the future for L. David Mech holds many more discoveries and excitement. He is looking forward to putting together all the data from the studies to tell the full story. He hopes eventually to write a book that will describe the interactions between the wolves and deer in Superior National Forest.

I hope I can help other people see the wolf for what it is: one more magnificent species, superbly adapted to contend with its harsh environment, and highly deserving of our understanding and acceptance

In *The Arctic Wolf: Living with the Pack,* Dave wrote, "I hope I can help other people see the wolf for what it is: one more magnificent species, superbly adapted to contend with its harsh environment, and highly deserving of our understanding and acceptance."

3

The Wolves of Isle Royale

IN 1949, THE ISLAND archipelago known as Isle Royale National Park received its first wolf population. Moose had swum to the island in the early part of this century and had lived there without predation for thirty to forty years. Logging along the North Shore of Lake Superior at the turn of the century had affected the populations of large mammals, first giving the moose an advantage over the caribou, and then the white-tailed deer over the moose. It was during their post-logging peak that some moose had swum to the island. Why they swam nearly twenty miles (32 km) in the frigid waters of Lake Superior is unknown, but their presence on Isle Royale is hard to mistake.

When the moose arrived they found the island to be one big chef's salad where they could browse and reproduce. This would have been fatal for both the stressed vegetation and the moose except for a fire that resurrected the vegetation and sustained both browse and browser for a short period. By the time the wolf crossed the ice from Canada to the island, the holiday was over for the moose. They had overproduced and overgrazed, and both plants and ungulates were in sorry shape.

Like the first moose, the immigrating wolves also found this island to be a bonanza, and the population grew from two (an educated guess) to twenty-four (which appeared to be an ideal number) and finally to fifty animals in 1980. During this period of wolf reproduction the moose became healthier. The population stabilized and then it soared again. Despite the increased predator base, the moose once again overpopulated the island, and the vegetation, which had just recovered, again faced the threat of overgrazing. Instead of an increase in wolf population, however, their number fell to twelve by 1989, and the age and distribution of those twelve did not bode well for wolf recovery.

Why did the population crash? Some said that the moose were now too healthy, but autopsies of the wolves ruled out starvation. Disease was, and still is, considered a possible cause as both Lyme disease and parvo-virus antibodies were found in wolf blood samples. The population crash of 1981–82 corresponded with a parvo-virus outbreak on the mainland of Michigan. Even though dogs are not allowed on the island, boaters still bring them over illegally, and the disease, which is primarily transmitted through oral-nasal contact, can even spread from dog feces on the bottom of hikers' boots. According to wolf researcher Rolf Peterson, "The big unknown is, Did disease cause the crash? Very likely it did, and we will never know."

There also is concern over the genetic diversity of the wolf population on the island. The entire population appears to be the offspring of one alpha female. If this is the case, the wolves may be losing 10 to 15 percent of their genetic variability each generation.

With the loss of population there also is a breakdown in pack structure and territories, which, in turn, raises the question, What does the national park do? "We decided we can learn more by letting it happen. The future looks bleak, but it would be bleak no matter what we did," said Bob Krumenaker, an Isle Royale resource management specialist, in a newspaper interview.

Isle Royale is an International Biosphere Preserve. It is an island free of roads and development, hunting and management. These facts guide the decisions that surround the wolf situation. But it is not an island truly free of human impact. It was a copper mine for Indians. Human impact on Minnesota's North Shore may have affected wolf and moose migration, and subsequent human impact on the North Shore of Lake Superior may preclude future immigration. If the cause of the population crash is parvo-virus infection, it is human related. It also is a human decision to declare these islands a national park. Vegetation on the island many support only one thousand moose and twenty-four wolves. Now there are nearly 50 percent too many moose and less than 50 percent of the potential wolf population. Isle Royale presents an opportunity to study the genetics of isolated populations and the potential extinction of a fragment of a species' overall population. The questions are, Why is this happening? and, Can we really just stand by and watch?

Rolf Peterson

Rolf Peterson summarizes the events that led him from camp counselor near Ely, Minnesota, to lead investigator of the Isle Royale mystery. "Dave Mech was Durward Allen's first graduate student on Isle Royale and I was his last. After Dave's research there was a whole string of people who emphasized different species on Isle Royale—beaver, moose, fox, and other small mammals. In 1969 [Durward Allen] was about ready to hang it up, but [he] said, 'Let's go one more round and get back to emphasizing the wolf.'

"Then things just sort of broke loose during my tenure. There really was a quite spectacular moose crash. I didn't have any frame of reference. Probably their population dropped by over half during the few years I was there. By the time I finished it was obvious that it was not time to quit. Wolves were really beginning to increase. Moose had bottomed out. The whole thing was really set up for change."

Rolf has the blond, Scandinavian look his name implies. He is not a large man, but he has the air of physical confidence that is shared with people who are self-reliant in wilderness areas. Reserved by nature, he is a good man for the field, where many hours have to be spent patiently collecting data and wrestling moose skulls out of tangled underbrush.

"By the time I was done [with the thesis], Durward was ready to retire, and he basically just turned it over to me. I had about a year's worth of funding to find another spot to base [the research] out of. Purdue didn't seem to be the right place for me, so I ended up at Michigan Tech. After making the local rounds here in the Lake Superior watershed at universities, there seemed to be more potential for landing a real job in Michigan Tech in 1975."

Rolf grew up in Minneapolis, Minnesota, and got most of his outdoor experience through YMCA programs. Canoe trips led him into the wilderness of Wisconsin, Minnesota, and Ontario, and through his college years he continued to pursue this interest. He first heard about Isle Royale through a newspaper article Dave Mech had written for a Minneapolis Sunday paper. Along with the article, Dave had a sequence of photographs at a fox den where one pup after another appeared, until there were five or six lined up at the entrance. Rolf cut the sequence of photographs out and hung it in his room.

Rolf wrote to Canadian wolf researcher Doug Pimlott about working on Baffin Island. When that didn't work out, he wrote to Durward Allen at Purdue. Allen was trying to figure out if he wanted to continue with the wolf study. He liked Rolf's canoe background, because it was similar to his own. Rolf meanwhile was debating whether to work on wolves or Lake Superior limnology, but when the Isle Royale opportunity came, there was no question whether or not he would do it.

"I'm pretty solid there now. But actually [that was not the case] until just the last few years. In '76, Dave [Mech] had this commitment to set up a project in Alaska on the Kenai Peninsula. He had to have somebody up there full time, and he was encouraging me to just kind of pack it in here and go out there. I just couldn't let go [of Isle Royale], although at the time neither one of us had any inkling of what was going to happen," Rolf says as he reflects on an event that could have changed both his life and our knowledge of Isle Royale.

"[On Isle Royale] moose had sort of declined and wolves were increasing, but the change wasn't that marked. I remember Dave asking me, 'Conceptually, don't you think you really have it pretty well figured out?' He was twisting my arm to just kind of drop it at that point. It didn't seem to either of us that we could see a real clear dramatic change coming. If I'd been right, in terms of my conclusions at the time, moose and wolves should both just sort of dwindled down and moose should have stayed down at a low level. . . . I'm real glad I hung on at that point."

That is an understatement. Even though Sigurd Olson began research in Minnesota in 1930 and Milt Stenlund followed with another study in the fifties, no place has had such a consecutive number of research years as Isle Royale. Considering the complexity of the current situation, that could be the most valuable aspect of all for those who have to make decisions about wolf-management policy today and in the future.

When Rolf returned to Isle Royale in 1979, after spending time on Dave's project in Alaska and teaching at Marquette, there was a three- to four-year period where the only financial backing for the studies came from private institutions. The number of wolves at that time was at an all-time high. Rolf explains, "At that point, even in 1980, we knew it couldn't last. I figured it would go down about as slow as it had gone up—five to ten years to bring the population back down to where the food could support it. Of course I was wrong there too. It just crashed. In two years they were almost all gone."

Rolf considers the situation. "Many of our cherished predictions and conclusions have been bad. We've thrown them out the window many times, but there are some that are real important that have just been solidified with time. The one that is probably the most important is selectivity of wolf predation for certain types of moose. It's more true now than it ever was. They are very selective predators. We've looked at two thousand wolf-killed moose, more wolf-killed moose than any other prey species in the world, and that's just as clear-cut as anything could be. Most of the moose in the population, the wolves just can't touch. Although a lot of our ideas about dynamics of predator and prey have gone by the wayside, that conclusion stands."

Rolf's research is very time consuming and it takes a patient wife to support such a project. Rolf's wife, Candy, has a degree in economics and history, as well as a teaching certificate. She was ready to go to the Peace Corps when she met Rolf. Instead, "I just attached my wagon to him and have been having a great time ever since. I was his field assistant when he was a graduate student and [I] typed his thesis five times."

Candy, an energetic and outgoing brunette, grew up in Duluth in a family that took camping trips in the Boundary Waters Canoe Area Wilderness. This background led her to be a camp counselor. She has been a Cub Scout leader and a Junior Great Books leader in her sons' elementary school. She is emotional about the wolves, the island, and the environment, and therefore, she may be Rolf's strongest supporter.

Candy relates how her role changed when Rolf went to Alaska. "[There] it was trapping and radio collaring and not just the slog through the muck, which is what we do on Isle Royale. I'm real good at that. When it became riding roads, watching trap lines, and flying in the airplane, I wasn't needed, so I tended kids, and I've been tending kids pretty much ever since.

"In the summer I've gotten more involved, but in a different way. We do Earthwatch studies, so I am the person who plans the menu and packs the lunches and checks everybody's equipment. It's a complicated operation, but I love that island and love those wolves." Candy plays an important role in the family and the research team, and she doesn't hesitate to offer her opinions either. "In meetings with all these scientists I'm always sitting there raising my hand to represent the aesthetic value of the island and the aesthetic value of unhandled wolves."

Candy speaks for many people when she reflects on her feelings, "The scientists are up there just going wild over what we could do if we could knock down these wolves every two weeks and take blood samples, and wouldn't it be wonderful, and they're all rubbing their hands. I'm saying, 'You can do that here with your captives.' Somebody has to stand up for them. There has to be someplace in the world where wolves can just be wolves. I think the thing we get out of the Isle Royale study is the relation between the wolves and the moose. Just slogging around in the woods and watching them from the airplane in the winter, there's a lot of data you can't get that way, and yet there's a lot of data you can get that way, that you can't get anyplace else in the world. That's the value of Isle Royale I'd like to see preserved."

There has to be someplace in the world where wolves can just be wolves

Of her family and their relationship to Isle Royale, Candy says, "I believe so much in what he is doing, that it's easy to sell our kids on it. 'Daddy's gone, but what Daddy's doing is a very important, good thing and be proud of him, and aren't you glad you're in this family. I just hope that you find something to do that you love as much. . . . He's very, very lucky.'"

For three months each summer, the family lives on the island. The Peterson's sons, Robin and Jeremy, have grown up on the freedom of the national park. Instead of TV and Nintendo, they grab old boards from the Park Service junk yard and make boats or create other fantasies. They camp, play, and learn that the wilderness is not alien to humans. It is in the wilderness and with the wolves that Rolf's professional concern lies. While his own family grows, his wolf families diminish. On Isle Royale packs were in the fifteen to twenty range during their peak. Now they are down to two or three animals.

Rolf works with the wolves in the ideal research situation: an island of 210 square miles (546 km^2) where only sixteen species of mammals have established themselves. The wolves' food pyramid consists primarily of beaver, moose, and hare. The mammals are not emigrating or immigrating, and there are thirty years of baseline data. Humans are on the island primarily in the summer months and they are restricted by national park rules.

Rolf has seen only five to six kills from start to finish. One time the moose tried to make a stand, failed, and ran downhill into a swamp and probably was dead in two minutes. It was a fifteen-year-old cow with severe arthritis. When she was first confronted, she was trying to kick just with her left leg; her right leg was too crippled by disease. The wolves were very quick to dispatch her.

Remembering the experience, Rolf says, "One of my favorite quotes of Durward Allen's is, 'All a predator really requires of its prey is that it stand still.' It's not the objective of the wolves to kill that moose, the objective is to get a meal. When wolves actually grab a moose, their objective is to immobilize it. They do this from the safest end, the rear. They attack the big muscles in the thighs in hopes of getting it to stop running. Then they often just sit back and wait. They're very patient. It's very safe. They sit, or stand, or sleep within range of that moose. They might even take a day or three or four. We've seen them sit there for seven days."

Rolf's conservative demeanor begins to fade as he describes his observations. "We never found [a den] until 1973. That was a big breakthrough for us. At that time the population was going up and the litters were big and noisy. They howled a lot. . . . Nobody had ever found a wolf den on the island before. Dave looked hard, but there may have been only one at the time he was there. They use beaver lodges on Isle Royale (also one pine stump and a hollow log). There's no soil to do very much with."

Over the years the researcher begins to think and feel a little like the animal he studies. "The beaches on Siskiwit Bay have always been heavily traveled. They always hit that beach. There are a lot of moose calves right there, and there's a moose lick right up the river. The wolves know where all these moose licks are." Rolf could add that, as the years go by, he too knows this information.

Researchers puzzle over food, genetics, and disease, but what if the entire problem was triggered by the female rejecting the alpha male? Studies on Isle Royale so far have given the world its most complete picture of natural mortality in the boreal forest. Researchers have collected moose skulls, and they have data from over two thousand animals. They know that after the age of seven or eight, moose teeth show wear and gum disease appears, arthritis shows up, and tapeworm cysts reduce lung capacity. Each of these problems affects the moose's health and vitality and, conversely, increases the wolves' opportunities to succeed.

Unlike observers on the mainland, until now wolf observers on Isle Royale have not needed to use traps and radio collars as the limited area of the island allowed for aerial census. The current crisis, however, has changed that as wolves are now scarce and hard to find.

Even with thirty years of data and observation this crisis could not have been anticipated. Rolf says, "The last twenty years have shown some violent fluctuations. Moose reached high levels, followed by wolf high levels roughly ten years later. This long-term cycle may last twenty-five to thirty years. Moose increased fairly steadily through the sixties to approximately 1,400 to 1,550. On the mainland, densities were five to ten [moose in a similar geographic area]. The stage was set for a big change. Wolf numbers weren't changing at all, but their spacing was changing. The large pack that Dave initially started watching slowly shrank. By 1971, the one big pack used less than half the island; the rest was vacant. Vacancies are usually quickly filled, especially if there's something to eat."

Continuing, Rolf says, "Beginning in 1969 there was a lot to eat, because of a series of four severe winters and lots of snow—thirty inches [75 cm] or more. This brought severe hardship to moose. Malnutrition made them very vulnerable to wolf predation. Very few calves survived at all. Most were killed in that first year. In late winter, wolves were often dancing on top of crusts that were up to the chests of moose calves, so calves perished in great numbers. The population of moose dropped by more than 50 percent by the mid-1970s. These were the golden years for wolves. Their numbers began to increase steadily. Additional packs developed. In 1972 a second pack formed. By 1975 a third pack developed in between the first two. In the late seventies a fourth and fifth pack were added. In 1980 the population stood at fifty, which was just an incredibly high density of wolves."

Rolf emphasizes how significant this number was. "In 1979, Sig Olson wrote a letter to me after he got the annual report that showed this increase. He was very concerned and suggested that maybe something ought to be done about all these wolves, that [the situation] was clearly getting out of hand. We didn't really know what would happen. It was clear by 1980 that there was severe nutritional stress among wolves. They were having a very hard time finding moose to kill, and something had to break. Pandemonium hit between 1980 and 1982. Spatially, the five packs were disorganized in 1981, there was extensive trespassing of packs onto their neighbors' territory, and fights ensued. By 1982 we couldn't even recognize any of the former pack territories or any of the packs. From 1980 to 1981, the population dropped from fifty to thirty, from 1981 to 1982 it dropped from thirty to fourteen. Over fifty-two wolves died during these two years [including new pups]."

Rolf pauses as he relays the events. "Finally in 1982, two wolves plus a couple of comrades took over the whole place. We called them the Gang of Four. They seemed to be enforcing the rules in Chinese fashion. Cleaning out the opposition. They didn't do quite a complete job. There were two pairs of wolves that remained. The Gang of Four eventually proliferated and became the dominant pack on the island. They had a pretty successful strategy to clean up the former overpopulation. I'm not actually sure they killed anybody. They were actively tracking down wolves, and it certainly looked like they would do harm to any interlopers they came upon."

Wolves often kill one another in territorial disputes and pack conflicts; however, there are other ways that they can dominate and eliminate competition. Packs can drive individuals off their kills and prevent the competitors from feeding. They can put stress on another pack by continually challenging for territory, thereby affecting the energy budget and hunting efficiency of the weaker pack. The social interactions are complex and many are still not known.

Rolf summarizes the chaos. "What I thought would take five to ten years was done in two years. Whenever our predictions aren't borne out, we usually learn something important. If everything conforms to your predictions you should be a bit disappointed, because you're not going to learn anything new. We were pleased to see that the population rebounded in '82 and '83 to about the same level it had been in the sixties, but it looked to us at the time as if we were just completing one full cycle of ups and downs in the moose and wolf population. We thought, 'If it went through that cycle once, it will repeat itself.' I think we've gone on a new track since that time."

Rolf shows a determination to follow this story whichever way it goes. "During that crash we picked up only five dead wolves. We wanted to know what the causes of death were. A lot of the old, single wolves, over 25 percent of that maximum pack population of fifty, died in that first year—all the loners. The marginal animals keeled over, basically. We found a couple that were very old, very malnourished. One old wolf had twelve broken ribs from a moose encounter that had healed. He had a cracked skull that had healed, and a broken scapula that had healed. He'd pretty much been through the wringer. These old-timers disappeared very quickly that first year. The second year, entire packs disappeared. Wolves were trespassing, chasing, and in some cases killing each other."

It is not possible to mark the point beyond which a species cannot survive

It is not possible to mark the point beyond which a species cannot survive, and the study on Isle Royale could be recording the elimination—or the recovery. In 1991, the annual report concluded: "The potential for wolf reproduction declined . . . as one of the four bonded pairs separated. With perhaps one exception, all of these pairs have previously attempted reproduction and failed."

Should we put wolves back on Isle Royale if they do disappear? It is a question that remains unanswered, but Rolf would hate to see the island without them.

Diane Boyd is a highly skilled trapper as well as an outstanding researcher. The wolves she studies roam the wilderness surrounding Glacier National Park on the United States–Canada border.

TOP INSET: *Rolf Peterson surrounded by moose antlers. Determining age and health of the prey species is an important part of studying a predator.*

MIDDLE INSET: *Fred Harrington studied the wolves in Superior National Forest to learn wolf howl language.*

BOTTOM INSET: *Over the years, L. David Mech has worked with most of the world's wolf researchers. Here he is with Luigi Boitani (left) of Italy and wolf behaviorist Erik Zimen (middle) of Germany. The photo was taken in the early 1970s, around the time Dr. Mech published his classic book* The Wolf.

ABOVE: *Running from a researcher? The wolf can travel for long distances if needed, but it relies more on pack cooperation than speed.*

ABOVE LEFT: *In the 1970s, an experimental attempt was made to reintroduce wolves to the Upper Peninsula of Michigan. A great deal of human animosity awaited these wolves, and within a few months of the transfer the four wolves transplanted from Minnesota were killed by either guns, cars, or traps. Jeff Renneberg, a research technician working with L. David Mech, is shown here loading a wolf into a plane for the flight to Michigan.*

ABOVE RIGHT: *Steve Fritts and Todd Fuller are shown here, early in their careers, weighing a wolf. Todd Fuller has left the wolves in Minnesota to become a professor at the University of Massachusetts, and Steve Fritts is now the wolf recovery coordinator for the western United States. He oversees the Yellowstone reintroduction program.*

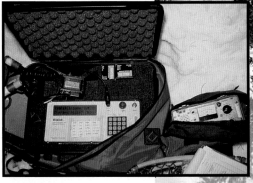

ABOVE LEFT: *Radio-tracking equipment is necessary for prolonged study of any animal that is not captive.*

ABOVE: *The Headwaters Pack from the air. This is one of the radio-collared packs that gives us important data on pack movement, interaction, and territory.*

OPPOSITE, BELOW: *Diane Boyd tracking Montana wolves. The use of electronic gear does not reduce the need to be in the field.*

4

Wolves of Alaska and Canada

THE NORTH AMERICAN continent has two major international borders, and they form distinct subdivisions in the story of the wolf. South of the U.S./Mexico line there is the possibility that the wolf has been totally eliminated, and its future is a political question. The United States between Mexico and Canada has pockets of wolf survival, with the only real success story being in Minnesota. In most of this area we are looking at reintroduction, natural immigration, and management. The heart has been taken out of wolf range, and expansion is limited by politics rather than biology. North of the Canadian line (including Alaska), the wolf still exists in a large natural range and, while it is not endangered, it does face reduction with the expansion of human development. In 1987, Canada's wolf population was estimated at 45,000 to 65,000, with 4,500 of these wolves in the Yukon, and Alaska had 5,900 to 7,200. Research in these areas comes the closest to telling us what wolf biology was like when the United States was one large tract of wilderness, and observes wolf and human interactions in areas of frontier expansion. Like their U.S. counterparts, Canadian scientists possess the technology to provide the kind of data we really need.

The issues that surround the wolf are often political, divisive, and

OPPOSITE INSET: *The radio collar is invaluable to the researcher and has helped humans learn much of what we know about the wolf.*
OPPOSITE: *Frozen waterways are a highway system for wolves in winter.*

obscure the search for knowledge. As this text was being written, Alaska promulgated rules for wolf management zones that would eliminate substantial wolf populations in some areas. It rescinded the directive after an outpouring of public sentiment against such an act. In addition, an Alaskan surgeon has been convicted of illegal airplane hunting. In Canada, two Ontario counties still offer bounties, and the British Columbia Wildlife Branch has used 799 types of poison baits. These actions will not be examined in this text, but they are symptomatic of the issues that have always been part of the northern wolf controversy. Our only hope of coexistence and effective management is increased knowledge and education. We must learn from the researchers and apply those lessons with wisdom.

Bob Stephenson

Alaska is a long way from West Allis and Milwaukee, Wisconsin, where Bob Stephenson grew up, but then almost all Alaskans, except the Native populations, have migrated from other states. Bob's outdoor-oriented family traveled, camped, fished, picked up sea shells, and enjoyed the rural and outdoor landscape. His father was an electrical engineer, and Bob describes his mother as a "housewife, birder, and ecologist lady."

Bob began college in 1963 at Wisconsin State University at Stevens Point, studying wildlife management. Professor Ray Anderson, whose background was in prairie chickens, took Bob and other students grouse hunting on weekends. They became good friends, and Anderson helped open Bob's mind to deer management and other wildlife issues.

Bob went from Stevens Point to a master's program at the University of Alaska from 1967 to 1970. Zoologist Bud Faye, who was with the university and the Institute of Arctic Biology, advised him on his research project. Bud had extensive experience with fox, walrus, and seals, as well as working with the Inuit. Bob reflects on Bud and other influences. "I've taken some refuge with people like Bud Faye and Dave Mech . . . who were big enough to withstand the fashions in wildlife thinking. The big swing is toward computers, and [people] mistake accurate measurement for science."

Bob is intense as he reviews his profession's history. He says that the mathematical model–oriented scientists had a period of ascendancy in the profession and looked down their noses at the old-style field naturalists. He explains that the mathematical models are hard to understand. Those who use them tend to focus on the academic side of things rather than on connections, and don't worry about clear and distinct written descriptions. "We became very cautious and weren't pushing and making connections. It was boring to a lot of people. I was lucky enough to have a couple of people who I could complain to about it, and they'd say, 'No, you're absolutely right. This isn't just measurement. It's thinking and making connections.'"

Bob's master's research was a study of arctic foxes on St. Lawrence Island in the Bering Sea. He spent the summer on the island with the Yupik Eskimo people. It was an interesting time of dens, big bird cliffs, the tundra, and the comparison of food habits. Bob describes the Yupik as "nice folks, not difficult people," who possess "lots of intelligence, humor, and generosity."

The National Guard took Bob to San Antonio, Texas, where he "did pushups" and "sweated a lot." Fortunately for him, a job opened up with Fish and Game in Alaska. It dealt with carnivore biology on the north slope of the Brooks Range and the northern part of the pipeline.

Bob describes his first wolf encounter. "I was resting on a steep hillside above the river, when I heard the soft thud of hooves on tundra and the clicking of joints of moving caribou legs. Five caribou ran past about twenty yards [18 m] from me, mouths gaping and heads low following a hard run. Seconds later, I spotted a light-colored gray wolf loping along the caribou's trail. It stopped briefly, gave me a surprised look, then continued its chase. Curious, I followed it, and after some distance I found a freshly killed caribou calf at the river's edge."

A side effect of this assignment was an introduction to the Nunamiut Eskimos through a fellow scientist. He learned that they knew of many wolf dens, and Bob wanted to find dens so that he could collect scats and learn about summer food habits. Bob says, "I didn't have a big budget. It wasn't a big program. I did a lot of walking, poking around, and camping out in those days. I decided I wanted to visit there and talk more with the people. This kind of field work was everything from playing cards, taking care of kids, helping out with flu epidemics."

Bob's eclectic interests helped him become part of the community. "I mean everybody was sick," he continues, "and I had some medical training. We gave babies cold baths to keep their fevers down, made people soup. It was a rough time. For several days we did whatever it took. There were emergency flights to the Native hospital in the middle of the night with people who were hyperventilating. We thought they had meningitis. But this was real involvement with the village, and when the time was right, and the people had the time, we tried steering the conversation toward wolves. And when it was good, it was good, and it might be an hour every day or two where it would really come out from somebody."

On a hot June day in 1970, he made the first of a series of stops. By the time he finished this work he had the location of seventy-two dens scattered around the Brooks Range. "It went on from there," Bob explains. "Talk about other things, about wolves, wolves and caribou, wolves and sheep, wolf intelligence, wolf whatever, and I pretty rapidly realized that these people had a special kind of experience with all those animals in that area, and that I should spend some time with them and try to learn."

Bob was fearful that this knowledge would disappear as the elders died. The lifestyle of the people had changed over time and the connection with the environment was not as strong as it had been. He convinced Fish and Game that it would be a good investment for him to spend time learning from them.

Between 1970 and 1973, he spent sixteen months living and traveling with the people. "We spent a few weeks each summer out watching for wolves in that open country, doing what they used to do, finding dens by observing wolves and deducing from their behavior the direction of active dens, and listening to them talk about what was going on. Bob Ahgook and Justus Mekiana were two people who spent the most time with me . . . [They] took me under their wing and liked to talk about animals. They are interested in what we know, and by and large their view of wolves is quite similar to the one western science has developed; but I think they have something to add to it, some good lessons we could learn about open-mindedness."

Bob's work and reading have given him the time and basis for reflection and philosophy. He says, "There is a lot of pressure on people in our research society, with the whole scientific mechanism of journals, and people committing themselves, as well as being subject to criticism. The Nunamiut just had to have their knowledge work for them. They didn't even have to defend it to the next person. It was an individualized kind of thing, but it was also collective. There wasn't all this pressure and competition to see who knows the most. They are just more low keyed about it. I think that was an advantage."

Bob illustrates this thought. "One morning we were trying to find a den to watch, not too far from Anaktuvuk Pass, which is the place they lived. We were just a short distance, about twelve miles [19 km], from the village, and there were wolves around, two dens that the Eskimos knew of from early days. Wolves can always make new dens of course, but their old ones are a good place to start.

"There was some activity there, but it was kind of quiet. We couldn't figure out which one they were using or if they were using either. We decided after a few days we would walk up closer. We didn't want to disturb it, but it didn't look like there was much going on. As we walked slowly up this little slope, Bob [Ahgook] said, 'There is a wolf trail.' Wolf trails have a certain look to them, a certain width and depth. They are not like the caribou trails that are kind of chopped up. These are just light, little trails. Then he said, 'There is a wolf.'"

Continuing the narration, Bob says, "It was a small gray wolf running up the mountainside away from all these big boulders. It's kind of a neat spot, with a golden eagle nest up above the den. This wolf ran up there and climbed through the rocks and disappeared over the top of this little mountain and escarpment, looked back at us, and then was gone. Bob Ahgook said, 'She has either had pups or is going to very soon because you could see that her abdomen was dark.' She had shed the hair around her mammaries. Then he added, 'The den must be up there.' I asked why, and Bob Ahgook said, 'Did you see that little bird?' I guess I noticed a bird, but he said, 'That bird, it was a robin, I believe. It landed and picked up some wolf hairs for its nest.' It had just flitted in and out, and he got all that information out of a little ten-second episode. I had seen the wolf and maybe saw the bird, but I wouldn't have known anything else really. We didn't even go up there because we didn't want to mess with it. We just left."

Bob was constantly reminded of the differences between his

upbringing and that of his companions. He relates, "You'd stop your snow machine somewhere and be sitting around and Bob would say, 'There's really a lot of brown rocks up on that mountain,' because he knows you don't see the caribou up there. They're a couple miles away and he has been watching them and seeing them for a long time and you are sitting there fat, dumb, and happy. It makes you realize that because they had so much country to look at, open country, there is a lot to see. And if you are busy with your eyes, you see more. They want to know what is going on, and they are good at it. We're not conditioned to do that much. We live in an inanimate world by comparison. It's closed in and we get a lot of information secondhand, through books or whatever. They didn't have any of that stuff. They had their eyes and their memory and stories and oral exchange of information.

"It's kind of interesting to realize that your eyes can really do a lot more than we think they can. And then the other part of it is, I think, that we are such an internally busy bunch of people, especially people in science or professions, lots of intellectual stuff going on inside. It is hard for us to tune that out and work on the external world with a clear head."

From these experiences Bob developed a respect for the Nunamiut that led to further study and interaction with the people of the far North. He concludes that "the people do not idolize the wolf, nor do they think of it with guilt or rancor." He also learned that the concept of wolves taking only the weak and inferior members of their prey is too broad a generalization. Weather, browse, snow depth, and the personality of the individual wolf all contribute to the selection of the prey.

Through the Nunamiut, Bob learned to judge the wolves as individuals who learn throughout their lifetimes. Wolves learn from failures and may even commit rather foolish acts. There are many who would question Bob's feelings about the wolves' individualism, but he is not afraid to voice his opinion. He says, "There's a fairly strong tradition that has a very bad name—anthropomorphism, a large sin in early biology. You're missing a good chunk of these animals if you can't accommodate that. The Eskimos never had any problem with it. They saw wolves as thinking animals, smart animals that learn, and an unavoidable byproduct is that they have a personality with no two exactly alike. There's a lot of similarity, and wolves do act the same generally. They live the same general way in a lot of places — they live in packs, they hunt big game, have a social order, but nowhere is it exactly the same.

"It makes it much easier to do what you will with animals if they are of a rank lower than people as far as sensitivities to pain, or trauma, or whatever. That was very common years ago. People would just do these insane, cruel experiments with animals, just to see what would happen. It didn't matter because they were just animals. I think there's much more ethics and consideration now in animal research. I'm glad to see it."

Bob reflects on some of the wolf individuals he has encountered. "I think of a young gray male wolf that we watched near Anaktuvuk Pass on a few occasions. He was really a sport. He snuck up on an eagle that was perched on a little glacier ice down on the river. He just walked up near it, and I can quite distinctly remember he did one of those movements with his feet. He made a little noise and the eagle looked around like, 'Oh, my God,' then flew off. He had a good time with that. He'd mess around with ducks in a pond, kind of walk around after them and make them swim. He climbed way up this mountain and slept in the rocks for the longest time, then came down in the evening just strutting his stuff, did a bunch of figure 8s, like, 'Boy, it feels good.'

"There was a young white male, he had the damnedest time making a bear chase him — a little grizzly bear. They were in and out of these willows, kind of playing tag, just running around. He had this play face on the whole time, just teasing this bear. There might have been a kill in there, but he wasn't too serious about anything."

Bob's manner is that of a person who has enjoyed his life, and he settles into storytelling with ease. "Then there was another little gray wolf, a male, that was just traveling with a bear. They were walking fifty yards [46 m] apart, and he just followed this bear. They would wander along together for a while going the same way, and if the wolf would get real close the bear might move at it a little bit.

"I watched a wolf sail a piece of dried caribou hide, a big chunk of it, probably from the Native people. He flipped that thing like a Frisbee, running around and catching it, just for a minute or two and then go on. Fooling around. They poke around a lot. The Nunamiut view the wolf as a highly intelligent predator that, with the sole exception of the occasional rabid animal, poses no threat to man. They are, in fact, quite amused by tales of bloodthirsty wolves lurking beyond the glow of the trapper's campfire."

Bob is a self-described "soft-hearted soul" who has taken in numerous stray cats and dogs. When he was young he always had a dog and also took in injured birds and squirrels. Although he describes himself as a shy person, and his choice of Alaska as a place to live attests to the fact that he does not like crowds, he is an exception to the many wildlife researchers who find humans incomprehensible and prefer to spend time with the "four-leggeds." "I guess I empathize with an awful lot of people. I understand strong egos, fears, and competition, but I am not a competitive person," he says.

Bob's study of both wildlife and the people of the North has continued since his early research activities. Following the decline of moose and caribou in the early 1970s, in 1975, he participated in the first large-scale study of wolf-prey relationships in Alaska that used radio telemetry. Using a dart gun fired from a helicopter, Bob's team radio tagged thirty-one wolves in fourteen packs. What he learned from this study was the extent of wolf travel. Almost one-third of the wolves made sudden movements of one hundred to five hundred miles (160–800 km). For Bob, this helped explain how wolves in Alaska and the Yukon can retain physical similarities and repopulate suitable areas quickly.

What we need to do now is stop the global march towards habitat destruction

From all of his work, Bob has come up with some strong opinions on the human-wolf relationship. "We kind of know a lot about wolves. We know what they need, we know how they live, but what we need to do now is stop the global march towards habitat destruction. Something that worries me is that if the U.S. economy goes to hell in a hand basket, and we become sort of a third-world country, we're not going to be as good about sharing with predators as we are now. We do it because we have the luxury to do it. The thought of a couple of hundred million hungry, desperate people scares the hell out of me. If they have the resources, they will probably not be willing to share with wolves. Those kinds of things are the real threat to wolves. It isn't whether you love wolves or don't love wolves, or whether you accept some wolf control or don't, or whether you accept hunting or trapping. Those are the realities of it. It's hard to make everything a national park and say just leave it alone."

Bob says with some pride, "I am outside a lot of mainstream work. I have always been a hybrid thing, involved in management stuff, a little public stuff, controversial things, helping pure scientists get samples, interested in a little of that, but dealing with a lot of weird samples of data and trying to make connections out of it. I worked on lynx for a while, and then back to wolves for a while. So I'm not really an academic person. I don't care to be. I kind of like the Renaissance man part.

"The pendulum is starting to swing back. You see it in the journals and bulletins, opinions about what the hell wildlife is all about anyway, and what are we doing. Kind of a reexamination." It is a reexamination that Bob is pleased to be a part of. Bob sees Lu Carbyn and himself as the people who hold the field naturalist position among the scientists. The advance of science, the discussions about genetics and varieties can't substitute for the observations of wolf life. It is only when we have an adequate amount of research on both ends of the spectrum that we will have a true picture of the wolf.

Wolf research needs to be long term, like the studies in Minnesota. We are continually being reminded that even the human lifetime is not long enough to really see the cycles and variations in the natural systems. In the long run it is less expensive to maintain a quality field research project than it is to start one up in response to a crisis, and it also provides a more accurate look at the situation.

According to Bob, "I think right now, shifting more towards public education and really taking part in this global crisis and the social change that's going to have to happen if we're going to persist at all is most important." In conclusion, he states, "I suspect the wolves will outlast us somehow, in the end, but if we want to have the luxury of this association with wolves, we're going to have to change something. There [are] a lot of potential dangers down the road. In the next few decades the decisions we make are going to be real critical. If we do not soon address these and other monumental issues, such as pollution and overpopulation, narrower issues in the debate over wolf management will be irrelevant."

Bob Hayes

In the early 1980s, moose populations in the Yukon were showing a consistently low influx of calves, and there was concern about overall moose health. This limited prey for both the human hunter and the four-legged predators. Bob Hayes was working on predatory birds in 1982 and 1983 when the town of Whitehorse experienced an increase in domestic animal predation by wolves. These events ran together, and the national press presented an image of wolves encircling the community.

Bob explains the incredible situation. "We had people from Europe writing about five thousand wolves surrounding the residents of Whitehorse, driving children up into trees and making them stay overnight." That October there had been twelve livestock-wolf conflicts. Normally there were three to four. A paranoia set in and kids were afraid to go to school, afraid to wait for the bus. Some parents would not let their kids play outside without a guard.

Why the wolves were so evident and attacked livestock is a difficult question. Although there are no hard data to support his view, Bob feels that part of the problem could have been the serious decline in snowshoe hares that winter. Hares have population cycles, and this was the bottom of the pattern. No fat wolf carcasses were found. With the moose population low, the loss of the secondary prey base added great stress for wolves.

Bob left Ontario the day after he graduated from Trent University with a biology degree. He and his wife were interested in living in the North, so they wrote to the Yukon about getting land, and at age twenty-two they took their child and moved to Whitehorse. Bob reflects on his traveling past. "My father was in the Air Force so we moved around a lot. I never really got to know any area, but I was always very interested in the outdoors. I lived for going out and hunting as a kid, then hiking and camping and canoeing. That was a really important part of my life." Bob's interest was developed with the help of two very close friends. Between the ages of twelve and fifteen they fished, hunted, and hiked a lot. Tragically, the two boys drowned in a canoeing accident.

Bob took his love of the wilds to the Yukon and let the fates provide him with opportunity. He remembers, "I was the only person looking for work in the summer. I got on with a bird person and we went into the Arctic. I continued with him for seven years. I became a permanent biologist specializing in bird of prey inventory. I was working in a group called small game when this wolf thing came up. We were working on bird carnivores, and they were looking for someone to look at some carnivore aspect. I was lucky." He was also in a difficult position. His job was to respond to the government edict to eliminate wolves. He was to be biologically sound, as well as sensitive to the people he lived with. The government wanted wolf numbers, plus information on what the wolves were eating. They opened a twenty thousand square mile (52,000 km^2) portion of the southern Yukon to private aerial shooting and trappers received a $200 "incentive" for wolves.

"The first thing I did is go to Alaska and contact Bob Stephenson, who has been very important in the design of the work in the Yukon," Hayes says. "We met Bob and spent three or four days going through techniques on how to study wolves in northern systems." Bob Hayes studied about three thousand square miles (7,800 km^2) of the Yukon and found a ratio of eight to twelve moose per wolf. There were few moose for the number of wolves in the area, and the data seemed to predict that the wolf was limiting the moose population.

"When we sat down and began to design what we wanted to do in there, there is no doubt that I agreed that in order to increase moose we needed to address bears and wolves," Bob states. "My responsibility was—if we are going to address wolves, let [the program] be designed so that we can learn as much about wolves as we possibly can. Many places that have had wolf control have not had follow-through with anything. We do not have any recovery information [after the control program]. We wanted to be involved in the design of that work."

Regarding the controversial aspects of wolf control, Bob says, "If you do not live in a system that has wolves . . . the death of one wolf is a major event. If you have five thousand wolves and you are removing wolves in an area that has 150 wolves, you are dealing with a very small area. It becomes not so much a biological question as an ethical question about reducing natural predators to increase prey so that people can hunt in low density. That is how you deal with low-density prey systems. That is what we have in the Yukon. Everyone believes that you go up in the Yukon and all of a sudden wildlife is much more abundant than other places, and in fact the reverse is true. The biomass falls dramatically."

Bob leans forward as he emphasizes his point. "We are dealing with things on the edge. You have systems that cannot handle a whole bunch of additional mortality. In our system, where you have so many natural predators, things are at a difficult stage for both the natural predators and the prey." Phrasing his thoughts into a question, he asks, "How do you plug into that in terms of people? They want to take some of those animals. Well, you have to be real careful with your natural predator considerations. They are the number-one takers of prey. They take way more than people do. We have two thousand of the most active hunters in the Yukon. We have four to five thousand wolves and six thousand grizzly bears. It is a natural predator system. That is the difficulty."

While others questioned the assignment's legitimacy, Bob set to work to define the potential. "My job then became, 'How do we remove wolves?' I got involved in designing the wolf-control work. We wanted to experiment with it. We wanted to do things like remove all the wolves but the alpha males in packs and see what happens. That occurred. We manipulated it ourselves and then [the government] caused the decline. We were involved in two years of wolf control. After three years there was still no significant bear reduction, so I proposed that continuing with wolf control in that area was of no value because we were not addressing calf recruitment. All the data that we could see showed that removing wolves was not going to increase calves."

Bob describes another northern area where they tried to increase calf recruitment through wolf control. "After three years they got no response. Using those examples we suggested that wolf control should be terminated. . . . From that point I switched and began to measure changes in the wolf population during recovery. The thing that I was really interested in was the predation rate data during the control period. I consider that to be really minimally modified by wolf control because the pack sizes were normal. We selected packs and did not remove wolves from them. Then we had a data set, following the control, to compare predation rates, to see if there was a functional response to lower pack sizes, larger territories, different age and sex structure of the wolves in relation to how they use prey. That was the continued portion of our study. We finished that in 1988 with the idea of a census every year."

Summarizing the results, Bob says, "[The wolf population] probably would have recovered completely in three years, but . . . we had a whole pack of wolves that were killed. . . . The alpha male was killed, the beta male ended up with the alpha female, and then he got killed. The alpha female was by herself with six pups. She ended up getting killed at a dump and all of the pups died. The population would have been 95 percent recovered if that pack had survived. In a normal population that had low exploitation, recovery would have been quicker. Being around Whitehorse there are a fair number of people that go out to do whatever they are doing and they shoot wolves at odd times. This time it was something that caused a very significant decline in the pack."

Bob has a second, more enjoyable study in northern Yukon near Peter Clarkson's study area. The problem here is the opposite of the situation in the southern Yukon. In this study they want to know why the ungulate population is increasing and why wolf numbers are at a relatively low density. Because of the size of the area, Bob spends most of his time doing aerial observations and very little time on the ground. While this is more impersonal than he might like, just because his work is done from the air doesn't mean that Bob hasn't built up his own list of adventures.

Bob tells us of one of his exploits. "We were darting a wolf. It was during a calf mortality study in the middle of the summer. Catching wolves in the middle of the summer is really hard because they are really difficult to hit. They are moving, they have all kinds of good footing, they are really smart, and they know helicopters. It is like they were born with an intuition to avoid helicopters or go to the side where the gun isn't. We picked up on a beautiful wolf. It was the oldest wolf we ended up catching. Beautiful, white male. We started pursuing it. We found it on a grizzly bear moose kill. The bear had eaten part of it and then slit open the belly and taken the fetus out. The cow was lying there completely uneaten except for a little bit along the neck where it was probably killed. We found the wolves and took off on our pursuit."

As he was preparing to dart the wolf, Bob accidentally hit the catch on his safety belt and ended up hanging out of the back of the helicopter with the door off and nothing to hold him in. He recalls, "The pilot is usually moving that machine, but this particular time when I was hanging out he did not move it at all. I was able to get back in, and I was really upset." Bob regained his composure, darted the wolf, and they landed ten feet (3 m) from it.

He continues, "It just stood up and looked at me square in the eye and ran away. I thought, 'Oh great!'" They pursued it again and seven or eight darts later the wolf was finally down, but so was the fuel. Bob told the pilot to get fuel and come back. Bob goes on. "I got all my gear out, and the wolf was laying there completely asleep . . . out cold. . . . It was probably one of the most striking wolves I have ever seen. His teeth were worn to little yellow knobs. He was thirteen years old—we pulled a tooth and found out what the age was. About twenty minutes into it, I was just getting the collar on. I had the wolf down and had all the hardware in my mouth. I had the collar around it, and I was just getting ready to put the nuts on. Then the helicopter comes back and makes a real loud noise."

Holding his hand twelve inches (30 cm) from his face, Bob says, "His head was right there. I feel him wake up and he is wide awake. He realizes something is really odd. There is something lying on top of him. I can see his eye and he looks at me." Reliving the experience Bob is visibly tense as he continues, "He exploded! I went reeling back ten feet [3 m] with my eyeballs going out like that, and the wolf went back the other way."

Bob also tells us how he watched wolves interact with their prey, "We followed this pack and it killed a calf moose, but it did not kill it right away. We got to it one afternoon. The calf was alive, and the cow was standing right above the calf. The wolves were eight to ten feet [2.4–3 m] away. There were five of them lying down watching. We flew around, and we could see that the calf was not dead yet. We thought it was going to be dead in a minute, and we watched. It didn't happen. They never did anything. We came back the next day, and the cow was still standing over the calf, with the wolves laying down right beside it. They hadn't moved more than ten feet [3 m]."

Shaking his head, Bob continues, "I wouldn't want to be within a half mile of that cow. She was just bristling. She was very distressed.

The calf was still alive. The third day we went back the calf was dead. We could see that it was not moving. The cow was eight feet [2.5 m] away from it, and the wolves were in the same spot. Three days waiting for this cow to move, and she would not move. She stayed there, standing over her calf. We came back the fourth day thinking they'd have eaten it, but they had left. They had given up on this calf."

Bob thinks about the people who have been part of his career and says, "Bob [Stephenson] has been a good sounding board for me. We deal with each other two or three times a year. He has a good understanding of the problems, the complexities, and a real love of wolves as well, which is very difficult not to develop when you work with the animals. Developing a respect for them is something that is going to happen to anyone, even the most ardent hater of wolves. Once they begin working with wolves they will understand what they thought about wolves is not true. Wolves have an amazing capacity to surprise you. Many people believe that wolves kill indiscriminately and all that stuff. When you've been working with them it doesn't happen.

"A good example would be our pilot, who is from Arizona—most of the pilots in the Yukon are American for some reason. When he started it was the 'dead, dumb wolves.' That's what he called them. He was pretty critical of wolves. He didn't hate them, but he was critical of them. He has flown for us for seven years now and his view of wolves has changed completely. He knows as much about wolf biology as I do in terms of what he has seen, and he . . . very much respects them."

Wolves have an amazing capacity to surprise you

Bob talks about the difficulty of balancing respect and predator control. "As you might imagine, being involved in a control program is really hard. In terms of your own personal kind of experiences, it's not fun. I went through a couple years of pretty long soul-searching about what we were doing."

Bob has had to take one of the hardest positions in wolf biology. Management is never a decision without consequence, and often the consequences are beyond our powers of prediction. The decisions that were made were not Bob's, but they are symptomatic of the conflicts that are going to continue to surface as human impact increases. How do governments balance the rights of wildlife with the demands of their citizens? The researcher knows that "to understand the true persistence, determination, and ability of a moose-hunting wolf, one needs to watch a single, hungry wolf at work." The persistence, determination, and single-mindedness of humans who want their way are reflected in the actions of their governments, and the researcher can only hope to add knowledge to the conflict between civilization and nature.

Lu Carbyn

Lu Carbyn grew up in Namibia in southwestern Africa but now lives in Canada with two daughters. He brings his African wildlife experiences into his work. As Bob Stephenson pointed out, Lu also stands out as a true naturalist—an observer. He has worked in Alberta's Jasper and Wood Buffalo, and Manitoba's Riding Mountain, national parks. His close association with the wolf in the field has added important anecdotal information to our body of knowledge.

While running the International Wolf Symposium in Edmonton, Alberta, Lu said, "I'm not at all ashamed of being a naturalist and having that approach to research, but really for one to make any sort of progress in learning more about the natural world, we have to go beyond just the observational stage. You have to quantify what you see and that means really getting a lot of data in order to be somewhat certain of your information. One or two observations will not do it. You have to repeatedly go out there and collect a lot of data and analyze that."

He says, "I started my wolf research in the Rocky Mountains in Jasper National Park. That was part of my profession. I was a biologist with the Wildlife Service and worked on my Ph.D. on the wolf-ungulate system, or predation, in a very complex system where there are several different prey species. I have some very fond memories of that study. I spent a lot of time up in the valley systems, watching wolves at the den sites, watching them interact with the different prey populations. It was very interesting. The wolves there preferred certain prey species that weren't necessarily the most abundant. As an example, mule deer populations were not that abundant, elk were, but the wolves preyed more heavily on the deer. Then, as the season progressed and the elk had borne their young, the predation shifted from deer to elk calves. That was a rather new finding. This research lasted three summers and two winters."

When asked to describe what the wolves in Jasper are like, Lu comments, "They're very free ranging. I've found them going right over ridges into the high country. They navigated over a snow cornice from one valley system to another. So even though it's rugged country, they find their way across various passes and travel a lot."

We wonder if wolves prey on high-elevation animals and Lu tells us, "They do, but it was very interesting. Certainly the big horn sheep were very lightly preyed upon. They have developed techniques to escape wolves by going to rocky ledges. The wolves just couldn't get to them in those areas. The main predation pressure was directed toward deer and elk. What happens in these mountain systems is you find that the major concentrations of game populations change the whole balance between the predator and prey. With a more dispersed prey population, the number of contacts per distance traveled by the wolves is far less than if they can find certain areas where they can come back and find prey predictably. It's a different dynamic."

Is Jasper a balanced system today? According to Lu, it is in a much lower equilibrium level than it was before. "At one time, wolves were quite heavily poisoned in Jasper National Park. When that happened there was an explosion of game populations. Then, as the predator control programs were lifted, the elk populations were reduced because of higher wolf predation. Now it's at an equilibrium that appears about a third of what it was." In a 1988 report Lu wrote that wolves occur in 80 percent of their former Canadian range. Seven of the ten provinces and both territories have wolves.

Riding Mountain National Park received its initial protection in 1906 as a Forest Reserve and as a National Park in 1933. As in so many national parks, development encroaches on all of the borders and makes the park a biological island. Wolves were a part of the ecosystem when the area was first homesteaded, but by 1900 they had been eliminated. In the early 1930s elk increased and wolves moved from Duck Mountain to recolonize Riding Mountain.

The history of this region is similar to that of other areas of settlement in North America. Once farming and hunting became established, humans and wolves began to compete, and the wolf was eliminated. Even within the park itself there were arguments that since elk, moose, deer, and beaver populations were important for tourists to enjoy the national park system, and since wolves preyed on these animals, it would be better if wolves were eliminated.

There is no statistical evidence that having wolves in the area has any detrimental effect on ungulate populations, which are controlled by food supply and disease. They have dramatic swings regardless of the wolf's presence. Studies have shown that elk numbers increased to levels of overpopulation in 1949. Moose have always been present and are increasing recently. Beaver declined most around the turn of the century when heavy trapping for the fur trade nearly eliminated them. Their numbers were so low that in 1947 and 1958 they were reintroduced into the area. Their numbers peaked around 1979. The beaver is not a primary food item but is an important buffer species that allows the wolf to maintain itself between larger kills.

During a study of the park's predator-prey system from 1975 to 1980, twenty-three wolves and a number of coyotes were radio collared. Warden surveys of ungulates and beavers were used throughout the study. Researchers determined territory sizes, animal distribution, and population numbers. Human impact was measured and management options that included various combinations of wolf and human involvement were examined. It was a significant study because it put the human factor into the biological picture, rather than treating it as a separate influence.

Lu says, "Regardless of any ethical considerations of how man should relate to animals, the fact that humans are a part of nature cannot be ignored, and the realities that include man as a part of the global ecology must be dealt with. Riding Mountain National Park is a good example of how man can influence an area, both in positive and negative ways. The park survived because man set it aside. Its wolves disappeared because of man's actions, and reappeared and survived again because of man's actions. Grizzlies are no longer a part of the Riding Mountain system, yet we rejoice in having the 'wolf wilderness,' even though it is without this copredator. Since man, the hunter, obtains his prey when it leaves the park, Riding Mountain National Park serves a spectrum of societal needs—the complete protection of nature on the one hand, and the production of game for hunting on the other."

Lu continues to philosophize from his naturalist perspective. "The greater and more diversified that human interests are in renewable resources, the better our chances will be of preserving the environment for future generations. For wolves, this can best be achieved if the predator can exist in natural areas of our modern world, free from the human-placed constraints of ethnocentric value systems—yet conservation should not end there.

"To say that mankind should not be an integral part of natural systems places humanity in a very artificial position—one that, if it persists, will ultimately result in the destruction of our planet. In my opinion, the simplistic views of extremists on either side of the 'wolf issue' demonstrate a lack of depth in their perception of the role of man in nature. It is in the role of responsible 'stewards' that humans will ultimately achieve the kind of relationship with nature that Aldo Leopold so eloquently espoused forty years ago, when he described his views of an appropriate 'land ethic.' "

Lu's next wolf study took him to Wood Buffalo National Park in Alberta. He describes the park with hesitation. "Wood Buffalo National Park is without doubt, in my mind, one of the most fascinating places on earth. If I praise it too highly, we'll have too many people come there and it will ruin the wilderness character of that landscape. It is unique. It's difficult to get into—it takes many hours by boat to get into the Peace-Athabasca Delta—and once you're in that area, you just see expanses of sage meadow,

> *To say that man-kind should not be an integral part of natural systems places humanity in a very artificial position*

sedge, and upland grassland areas, and in those meadows we have large populations of bison. Associated with these bison are the wolves. The scene certainly looks very much like the great plains at one time, when there were thousands of bison ranging over large areas in contact with wolves."

The herds in this area represent a remnant of the woodland bison (or possibly hybrids of woodland and plains bison). Lu says, "The taxonomists certainly debate this. Some have said the woods bison is quite different from the plains bison and has different characteristics, while others say they're the same. The genetics are crucial in determining whether an animal population belongs to the same group or another group. The genetics are not clear at this date. They do appear to look different. A woods bison is bigger and darker in color.

"Their numbers have suffered in recent years and the wolf was once thought to be at fault, but research has uncovered a more insidious enemy — brucellosis and/or tuberculosis." In Mackenzie Bison Sanctuary, the rare woods bison are expanding rapidly in the presence of a healthy wolf population and the fear is of contact between the two herds, not wolf predation.

To study the wildlife, Lu is using Doug Pimlott's habituation model, which is to find rendezvous sites and just sit and observe. This can mean staying in one place eight to ten hours at a time. Wolves have come as close as fifteen to twenty feet (4.5 to 6 m) from Lu before detecting him. These wolves are completely removed from humans and have not developed the fear inherent in other populations. A similar situation exists in Denali National Park in Alaska, where wolves are exposed to humans — but not hunting or trapping — making them more visible to tourists than in any other park.

Lu mingled with both bison and wolf and got so close he could touch both. He relates, "I'm certain both the wolves and bison are aware of my presence. I have found on occasion that they would respond to my presence, but I just don't get the impression that my presence is much of a problem. They seem to go about their business as if I wasn't there. You never try to push them, so you establish your base camp near where the bison or wolves are. The wolves find out you're there very quickly and seem to pretty well accept you. There isn't any indication that there's a big change in their attitudes towards the investigator."

In the summer of 1980, Lu studied bison cow-calf interactions, calf-pod formations, and wolf predation attempts from a tower in the middle of a meadow. In 102 days, he observed 166 encounters between wolf and bison. In only 2 percent of these encounters was there an attack.

Lu describes the wolf-bison interactions. "Wolves will intermingle with bison and very often the bison completely ignore them. . . . When a wolf pack is serious about an attack, the bison seem to respond very quickly. They can discern the intent of wolves. Normally, you'll see wolves lying ten to fifteen feet [3 –4.5 m] away from a bison calf and nothing will happen. You'll see three, four, five wolves in amongst the bison, and it seems to be a very peaceful scene."

We asked if there is a physical clue or what creates the change, and Lu says, "They're very intent when they're about to attack. . . . There's a body language that's pretty clearly discernible. The bison notice that too. They become more alert, the tail goes up, and they become alarmed."

Asked if he found the pack working together and singling out an individual, Lu says, "They will . . . zero in on one potential victim in the herd, then concentrate on it. There will be a lot of bison running in all directions. . . . On some occasions they will try to protect their calves by attacking, but normally they will flee. They are sort of in a disoriented mode and then one of them becomes a victim, because that's the one the pack will zero in on. Wolves . . . have a very strong search image for calves . . . in the summer and early part of winter. But these packs will kill cows and bulls, depending on the time of year."

Lu captured the drama of the hunt in his paper "Descriptions of Wolf Attacks on Bison Calves in Wood Buffalo National Park." The following is a summary of that account.

On May 28, 1980, at 6:20 in the morning, one cow and young calf were resting when the researchers spotted four wolves. The wolves were not trying to hide. At 7:00 A.M. the bison got up to graze and dispersed. The wolves moved in on the cow, and the calf began to run. The wolves circled the bulls, while the cow and calf sought refuge among five of them. One wolf lunged at the calf, and the other three wolves followed in chase. The five bulls surrounded the calf and tried to attack the wolves. This lasted only a few seconds and then the bison moved to higher ground. One bull charged the wolves and the others closed in around the cow and calf. The wolves withdrew to a sedge area and lay down.

At 8:30 A.M. the second attack took place. One wolf initiated the movement. The cow turned away the lead wolf, but several wolves grabbed the calf and pulled it down. The calf struggled free and the cow returned with several bulls. The calf stood pressed against its mother's side. Once more the wolves were turned back by charging bulls, and after fifteen minutes, the cow, calf, and three bulls were back in the main herd with the bulls lying down and ruminating. The wolves rested too. This was the first pause after three hours of conflict.

Then the alpha and two other wolves moved past the bulls toward the cow and calf, but they were thwarted when the original three bulls, plus seven new bulls from the herd, drove them away. At 9:15 A.M. the wolves attempted to stampede the herd but failed, and the cow and seven to eleven bulls kept the wolves at bay.

The cow and calf grazed, moved, walked around a ridge, and reacted to numerous feints. The calf continually fell behind and had to be moved along by its mother. Finally the calf fell behind, drew the wolves, and suffered a fourth intense attack.

The calf ran to the mother and the cow turned to defend it. The calf was knocked down, but scrambled to its feet and fled to the ridge, leaving the wolf with the cow. A single wolf continued the chase, but a bull intervened. The cow struck the wolf with its forefeet and the wolf rolled over, came to its feet, charged past a young bull, and almost caught the calf descending the ridge. It was joined by three more wolves, but met three bulls surrounding the calf. The cow and first young bull drove them off.

At 10:30 A.M. the wolves made another charge that failed. The cow ran and the calf followed. Three more bulls came forward, but the wolves went by them and overtook the calf. The alpha wolf grabbed the calf for the fifth time, but was chased off by two bulls and a cow. There were numerous charges by both sides with no contact, then two wolves broke through to the calf and downed it for a sixth time. It still had the strength to squirm away and run off, but three wolves pulled it down for a seventh time, only to be chased off by the adult bison. The wolves were excited and circled and darted in and out looking for an opening.

The alpha grabbed the calf an eighth time and was chased off by the cow. The calf rose much more slowly this time, and the cow and calf had to avoid several charges as they trotted off accompanied by one young bull. It appeared as though the wolves were tired when the herd gathered near an aspen bluff. The wolves moved into the tall grass but sprang up and gave chase as soon as the two bison moved off from the group. Two bulls wheeled to charge as the wolves overtook the cow and calf. Two wolves grabbed the calf and took it down by the hind legs. This was the ninth time, but still it kicked free. Three bulls came up in defense, and the five bulls left in a tight formation.

At 11:05 A.M. the wolves attacked again, and the cow and calf bolted from the herd. The wolves saw them separate and charged, but were rebuffed by four young bulls. The bison and wolves were at a stand-off until more bulls charged. For the tenth time two wolves succeeded in grabbing and taking down the calf, but once more the wolves were chased off by the cow and a bull. The calf scrambled to its feet and ran to a sand ridge. The pack caught up, but the bulls intervened. Five hours had elapsed since the initial attack.

From 1:30 to 4:30 in the afternoon, the bison rested, then the cow got up to examine the calf's wounds. Within fifteen minutes the alpha wolf was up too and trotted in a straight line toward the bison with the rest of the pack behind.

The cow and calf made a quick dash from the bulls to the herd, and the alpha wolf gave quick chase only to be thwarted by another bull. The wolf was so intent it appeared to leap over the bull's rump, but cow and bull shielded the calf.

At 5:30 P.M. a subordinate female wolf rushed the calf. Another bull deflected her. At 6:00 P.M. another attack knocked the calf down for the eleventh time, before the wolves were turned away and finally abandoned their quest.

Just as Bob Stephenson lamented, we have too few field naturalists to give us the vivid details of life and death, species' interactions, and the complexities that are part of our ecology. Through observations, Lu fills in the gaps that exist in understanding the great bison herds of North America and the free-ranging wolves that moved among their prey. How different is the hunting and stalking when the prey is abundant and cover is almost nonexistent.

Through these glimpses we see details. We learn that in a stampede the young are in the first third of the herd with the bulls in the back, but when the herd crashes through the brush, the vegetation acts as a filter that pushes the calves to the back. Lu tells us of bison dying as they crash through river ice without the influence of the wolf. We learn that the story is not a simple wolf/bison equation. Nature is too complex for us to put in simple models. In this study we learn about nature beyond the human influence, and perhaps we can learn the greatest lesson of all—nature does not need humans to survive or function.

Peter Clarkson

One of the things that has most impressed Peter Clarkson during his study of wolves is their resilience. He says, "They are so hearty. They . . . make their living by killing and traveling. The more they travel, in a sense, the more they can kill." For Peter, wolves are survivors.

But it isn't just their hunting that has impressed Clarkson. He adds, "They are efficient killers, with one wolf being able to pull down a moose or a caribou. That in itself is quite incredible. Seeing that, and then seeing the contrast, with an alpha male having his ears and tail pulled by a whole pack of pups. That kind of hardness of a very evolved killer, to something very soft and gentle and understanding."

Peter's enthusiasm for his work is evident. "There is always something exciting happening with the different packs, and watching the packs split and rejoin, and even visiting." His study area in the Northwest Territories of Canada covers 58,000 square miles (150,800 km²). Some of the wolf packs can cover more than 11,500 square miles (29,900 km²). They can travel twenty to thirty miles (32–48 km) in a day. It is such a big area that to get to the middle takes two hours by small plane; to reach the other edge of the study area takes almost five hours. Peter says, "It is difficult to appreciate until you have actually seen it and flown over caribou for thirty minutes."

Wildlife conservation, particularly the area of people and wildlife conflict, was the area that interested Peter when he was an undergraduate at a small college in Missoula, Montana. His initial focus was on bears and bear education programs, but while working on his master's at the University of Calgary, Alberta, there was a lot of controversy over wolf management, and this is what he chose for his master's work.

In graduate school, he wrote his thesis on wolf management and a booklet called "Bear Essentials," which was a reference book and planning guide for teachers and interpreters who had to give safety and bear education programs. After spending two years in the field in Alberta studying wolf-elk ecology and three years looking at bear-people conflicts in the Territories, his present research job opened up. It is a study of wolf-prey relations—in this case a large migratory caribou herd—and general wolf ecology, with no management considerations. Peter has found the results from this study exciting.

The project was initiated at the request of the Native people of the western Arctic, the Anuvik, whose Game Council and Wildlife Management Advisory Committee direct the research done on their land. They chose the wolf-caribou relationship program because they harvest caribou as their main food source. They also trap and hunt some wolves for clothing and sale of the pelts. Showing considerable foresight, the Anuvik wanted to better understand the system, what happens within it, and what impact they're having on it. They funded the project from their land claims money. The cost runs somewhere around $150,000 per year, which includes the salary for two researchers.

The attitude of these Native people toward wolves is very different from that of people in other, less remote areas. There are no tales of Little Red Riding Hood in their culture. Peter tells us, "The people spend a lot of time on the land, and I think they can relate very closely to wolves, because in a traditional sense the wolves and the people were after the same type of things. A good hunter, or a good family, was like a wolf pack. They were able to survive by hunting. . . . A lot of them respect how smart wolves are. The hunters are very interested in how wolves hunt and other biological information. No one is very concerned that if they go out on the land, they could be eaten by wolves.

"The wolf also has a very strong spirit among the animal spirits. It would get more attention and reverence than some of the other species. At one time there would have been a much more sophisticated ceremony for harvesting wolves, but there is still a lot of respect in the communities for wolf hunters. It is like being a polar bear hunter. It is something that not just anyone can do. You have to be a very good hunter or a very good trapper to be a wolf hunter, even with the more mechanized means. It still is much harder than hunting caribou or some other animals."

Even while Peter has seen the Native peoples' interest in and lack of hatred for wolves, he is well aware of the strong emotions the animal elicits in other people. His father is a farmer and to Peter's knowledge he has never seen a wolf—yet. He tells us of his father's reaction to his work. "We would call him on the phone and tell him that we came back from the field and caught thirty wolves. He would say, 'Well, what did you do with them?' I would say, 'We collared them and released them.' He could not understand that. His response was, 'Why didn't you knock them on the head?'"

Peter thinks the great dislike and fear of wolves relates to competition. "It's like the way people feel about other races. There are very strong emotions about minorities because of the competition. People are afraid that they are going to come in and take jobs. It is the same argument with wolves. They are going to come in and kill our livestock and kill our livelihood."

Working with wolves in the far northern region has given Peter opportunities to observe them and learn to admire them in ways similar to the Native people. Showing his enthusiasm, he says, "Wolves are always so much more exciting [than bears] to study because they are always doing something. There is so much pack structure, . . . and you have got so much more social interaction. There are going to be new pack members, or perhaps some of them have left the pack, or some of them may have died. They could be chasing something, or killing something, or resting. They are so individualistic. It is almost like the study of people. You get some wolves that are helping out all the time. Other wolves just laze around. Some wolves go off traveling. Other ones keep to themselves. Even within a pack you get real different personalities."

The great dislike and fear of wolves relates to competition

One pack of four the researchers monitored in Alberta had a dominant female with a broken leg. Even from the air it was quite evident that her rear left leg was broken, because it stuck straight out to the side. They never captured her to determine how it might have happened, but she was not using the leg at all. "We were expecting the pack to . . . turn on her and kill her, or she would be left behind on her own and not be able to keep up with the pack," Peter says.

One time they saw the pack moving across some deep snow. It was in the open so they could see them easily. Peter relates what they observed. "Three wolves were ahead of her. They went a ways and crossed this open area. She was just starting to come across. The third wolf at the end looked back at her. They could see she was having a tough time in the snow. He went back probably about twenty-five to thirty yards [22.5–27 m] and met up with her almost as if to say, 'Are you okay?' The wolf turned around again and went on the trail and she followed it back to the other wolves. There was almost an 'I'll be okay' and off we go again. She stayed with the pack for the entire time that we were studying them."

The following summer it appeared that she had pups, because she went off by herself in the spring and remained pretty much by herself for the entire summer. The researchers saw her with a pup in the fall. This same wolf also went from that pack over to another pack probably ten to fifteen miles (16–24 km) away on what appeared to be a visit and then returned to the other area. "She was very independent. She never did regain use of that leg. On three legs she lived quite well," says Peter with some admiration.

One of the things that Peter and his fellow researchers have discovered in the Northwest Territories is a seeming lack of aggression among packs over territories. He tells us, "We have had situations where two or three packs would be quite close and making different kills. From what we could see there was no aggression between them." In one area there was a chain of three lakes, and here they caught wolves from three or four different packs. Describing the wolves, Peter says, "There is no advantage to them fighting over these areas. For one thing there is a lot of food, and there is no sense in protecting these three lakes because tomorrow there may not be any caribou and then they [will] have wasted their time. You are much better off to keep going with the caribou."

It is here, around the lakes, that they have been able to observe some of the pack dynamics. There are some very large packs in the area, and the wolves sometimes split off to join other packs or to form new ones. "We would have just about every wolf collared," Peter says, "and follow them coming into that system, and then see who they left with when they were going out. . . . In one case, one wolf was with the pack for over a year and all of a sudden with another adult reproducing wolves. Somehow he joined up with another pack. How was he able to join them and travel with them?"

While caribou are the main prey of the wolves, musk oxen, moose, Dall sheep, and bison are also available. Small prey include hare, lemming, moles, muskrats, a few beaver, and some birds. On one occasion the researchers located a pack and noticed that the alpha male was carrying something in his mouth. Peter says, "The other wolves were coming in and wanting a piece of it. We couldn't tell if it was a piece of leg or what it was. He was very protective of it. He must have just caught it. . . . After fending off a couple of the younger wolves, he took it down onto the lake and dropped it on the ice. That is when we could see quite clearly that it was a muskrat. He then proceeded to eat it."

One of the early questions the researchers hoped to answer was where the wolves denned. Would they go to the caribou calving grounds where there was a lot of food for a little while? The pups would not have been mobile before all the caribou left the area. They discovered that most of the wolves chose to den in about the middle of the caribou range, below the tree line. Here they can get the caribou coming through on the summer migration and back again in the fall.

In order to follow the wolves and learn more about their pack structure, the project has included radio collaring. This has led to some interesting discoveries and exciting moments. They thought one female they collared was by herself all summer. They didn't see her until the following spring when she was with six other wolves. Thinking she'd finally joined a pack, they captured her, replaced her collar, and then caught four of the other five wolves. They discovered all of these were pups. She had raised an entire pack of pups by herself. It's most likely that her mate was killed by a hunter right after the breeding season.

Peter shares her story with us. "She had been a single parent to this whole pack. We never saw the pups because whenever we would come to locate her, she would take off running and would be two or three kilometers [1–2 mi] ahead of them. We would see her, and she was always by herself." After they collared the pups they discovered the same thing. Every time they located her, she was by herself, usually running through the trees. All of the pups would be trotting about a mile (1.6 km) behind her.

Capturing an entire pack and collaring all of them at the same time is something the researchers do in order to determine who is who and the ages of the pack members. It provides important information about pack structure. Peter explains. "In some cases where we have taken down an entire pack . . . you may have some of the first ones done, but it may take a half to three-quarters of an hour to bring in the last ones. We have had situations where we are working on one, and just a few feet away another one is already sitting up watching you and what is happening. Often I will pull them off a ways, so there is less stress on them and they can watch from a bit of a distance. Then they will get up and walk away."

Peter continues, "One time we had to wait with the helicopter because we were out of fuel. We had done everything and were watching them all starting to get up. This one got up and started walking toward the helicopter. The pilot was a little bit concerned that he not walk toward the tail rotor. I got out thinking I would walk towards him and he would run away. He just stood there looking at me. He stood there like the family dog would. I walked up and touched his nose with my boot. He blinked and pulled his head back a bit, but was still not going to move. He didn't seem aggressive so I walked up and stood beside him. He half looked around. Then I grabbed him by the scruff of the neck and the rump and lifted him up. His legs kind of went straight. I carried him about fifty feet [15 m] and set him back down. He looked around a bit and I got back in the helicopter." Laughing and shaking his head at the memory, Peter adds, "It was incredible. No aggression at all."

The experience of collaring does make some wolves more leery of the planes flying over, while other wolves seem not bothered at all. "They are very afraid of the helicopter, but most of them are not afraid of the fixed-wing plane. A couple of females are very sensitive— they are much more agitated, they want to get out of there, get off the lake—while the others could care less and are just lying around.

"I remember one occasion when we flew over and I thought, 'Oh no, we have a dead wolf.' It was a dark wolf. We could see him lying on the lake stretched right out. We flew over—we were probably fifteen to twenty feet [4.5–6 m] above the ice—and he did not move.

We flew over again. We were just about ready to land, when we flew over the next time and I saw his head flip to one side as we went over. We flew over again, and he watched us, wondering, 'What are these people doing?' He was not going to get up. All we saw was his head move. Then he sat up and did a big stretch, looked at us, and sat down and watched us for a bit."

Peter has learned not to fear the wolves, but the hazards associated with locating and observing them have given him some hair-raising moments. "Doing the capture work we are always on the edge, because you're flying in a helicopter, you are going, in some cases, sixty-eight miles [109 km] per hour, from two to ten feet [.6–3 m] above the ground. The pilot is focusing on the wolf to get you into position, while at the same time watching for trees and snow drifts, or whatever. In my position in the helicopter, being the shooter, I am hanging outside the window concentrating on the wolf, not even thinking about where we are going.

"There have been cases where we have come in and we are chasing wolves into open areas, or trying to catch them as they cross lakes. The helicopter will come in very quickly, especially if it looks like the wolf is heading off the lake towards the trees. I have been hanging out the window just about ready for a shot and out of the corner of my eye I catch a tree coming and I have to lift up and the tree goes by, or I'll be hanging out the window concentrating on the wolf because it is a small target and it is running full out—thirty miles [48 km] an hour. The helicopter is moving, trying to get an aim on that. I have total trust in the pilot, and all of a sudden I feel the helicopter pulling way back. If you were not tied in and leaning on the window, you would easily flip out. Then feeling the helicopter pull back and lift up, all of a sudden there are trees going underneath. It's quite an adrenaline rush."

Further illustrating the hazardous nature of his work he adds, "We've had a couple of times when we had been chasing some wolves on the lake where afterwards the pilot has said to others, 'I could hardly pull it up and we were just about to go over.' You think, 'Holy Jesus, it's not that important that we stop that wolf. We'll get it five minutes later.' [With] all of that flying, any kind of mechanical problem would mean a serious accident, if not death. You would be driven into the ice or . . . " His voice trails off as he finishes the thought for himself.

There have been close calls. One winter they were out picking up wolf carcasses that trappers had gotten but not taken to town. They had already made three landings and were coming in for another. The snow looked good, there didn't seem to be any problems, when all of a sudden the front nose wheel broke through the snow and the plane started going down. Peter says, "You could feel the back of the plane coming up. The prop was still turning. All of a sudden we were looking straight into the snow and everything was white. It wing-tipped and that prevented us from flipping right over. My immediate reaction was, 'Let's get out of here.' The pilot was a bit shaken up, but nothing was damaged. The first thing you think of is 'boom' and things burning up. You don't know what kind of damage has happened when you went half over.

"I just wanted to get out of there. I'm buckled in but ready to get out. The pilot is sitting there looking at things. Finally I said, 'Well, we might as well get out and look.' There was no door on my side. I had to wait for him to get out. Finally he got out and so did I. We looked it over, there was no fire or anything, but I just felt much more comfortable being out of it."

They have never had a fixed-wing plane go down, but Peter was on one that just about did. It was on a monitoring trip. They landed on a strip that was not quite ready for use, but they had pushed their fuel to the limit and had no choice. They had taken out most of the trees preparing the landing strip, but there were still some two-foot (half-meter) willows. They landed fine and put in some fuel, then they prepared to take off again.

"I had the feeling that he didn't let it rev up high enough," Peter says, "but we had started rolling. We passed the spot where we needed to be in the air. We were getting up speed, but the willows were catching us and slowing us down. Pretty soon we were past the end of the runway. There were trees lying on the ground—it was quite rough and bumpy—and then all of a sudden we are just getting into the air and there are some of the trees. 'Bang!' we hit one tree and the plane tilted a bit. 'Bang!' the plane hit another tree. You can see the flag off the wing. It is torn and flapping in the wind. We hit the two trees on one side. I am looking out that way to see how badly the wing was damaged. I turned around and there was a forest of trees ahead of us. The pilot turns so that we are barely missing them.

"I thought for sure we were going to catch the wing tip and go down. Somehow, and I still do not know how, he managed to gain some speed. As soon as he would start turning, he would start falling off and the wing did not catch anything else. Then he straightened it out and missed a couple of other trees. Then we were up into the air. He was just swearing by this time. I am sitting in the back, glad we are alive. Then the sweat came. Both of [us had] legs like rubber. Needless to say, we did not land there again."

Working in the remote regions of the world means that you not only face danger frequently, but you make do with whatever is available and continue on with your work. With an air of nonchalance, Peter concludes the story. "We landed at another location and patched up the wing. One dent was a fairly good one, and the other one we were able to pop it back out. Then we took a garbage bag and filled it with moss, and stuffed it in the hole and taped over it. We then continued to fly for the next two or three days."

The Canadian biologists bring us closest to wildlife beyond human influence. They also take us the farthest into areas we would call wilderness. The events that are part of their daily lives are adventure to the rest of us. They live in frontier land where they must be like the animals they are studying—adaptable and accepting of all conditions. Through studies like this, we can begin to eliminate some of the myths of the bloodthirsty behavior of wolves and see wildlife as an element of a broader palette of life and form.

> *Through studies likes this, we can see wildlife as an element of a broader palette of life and form*

John Theberge

John is a college professor and protégé of Doug Pimlott. In the United States and throughout the world, Mech is the symbol of wolf knowledge and research, but in Canada, and in particular for John, Doug Pimlott was the father of wolf research. He was the force behind the Canadian Nature Federation, Canada's largest conservation organization. Pimlott also started the Canadian Arctic Resources

Committee, which represents the north country's people and land against government and industry, and he was a founder of the International Union of Conservation of Nature (IUCN).

John grew up as a naturalist and bird watcher. As a kid, he started a naturalists' club, and in high school he applied for a government job. It was his good fortune to be assigned to Doug Pimlott. He went on to do a master's degree under Pimlott at the University of Toronto. After completing his Ph.D. in British Columbia, he worked with Pimlott as a colleague until the latter's death.

Doug Pimlott was John's intellectual benefactor. Reflecting on Pimlott's philosophy, which he shares, John says, "He was an advocate for the protection of wilderness and large chunks of land, the natural evolution of being. If you're concerned about these mammal systems, then pretty soon you ask, 'Where are they going to exist in the world in the future?' They aren't going to exist by default. We have to do something. And I guess I follow the same way. As a student of wolves, now I spend equal time in conservation lobbying."

Algonquin National Park in Ontario is John's primary study area. It is a land of lake-studded boreal forest, and it provides John with the biological background for his ideas. His study is an ongoing look at wolves in a national park that has great similarities with the Boundary Water Canoe Area Wilderness/Quetico Provincial Park area of lakes and forests. The study has continued the work of Doug Pimlott, who finished his studies in 1965. It represents an important look at wolves in a large and isolated Canadian wilderness complex that is surrounded by major roads and human development in the populated eastern Great Lakes region.

John's training as a wildlife manager gives him a professional background in a field that seldom endorses wolf protection. His wilderness philosophy recognizes that to let the species alone can be a sound management decision. "I gave a speech in Vancouver that was the most heartfelt I have ever given," John says, "because that's the one place where I stood up in public . . . and opposed wolf control in any form, even in livestock situations, and I'm only one of two biologists who have ever done that."

John wrestles with decisions like the Yukon "study" that Bob Hayes was involved with. He feels that the Yukon Territorial Council reacted to the emotional plea of an outfitter who claimed that the wolves were killing all the big game. The result was a decree from the government to the Wildlife Branch that John describes like this. "We're going to kill wolves. You've got six days to write a proposal and make it look good."

His willingness to take issue with government and other wolf biologists doesn't always endear him to his contemporaries, but it is important that someone steps forward to challenge ideas and decisions. He has written a study called "When is Wolf Control Necessary?" with the hope that it can be a manifesto for Canada and the world. There is a long way to go before his ideas are adopted.

Many scientists view their study species with an attitude that forbids emotional attachment. Sometimes this detachment actually causes them to take stands that are politically correct but avoid advocacy for the animal as though such support were criminal. John does not avoid working for environmental organizations like World Wildlife Fund Canada, and he is not above confronting his colleagues and government over issues that he feels are antiwolf. He sees the wolf as an intricate part of a natural ecosystem and does not agree with artificially controlling their populations through bounty or government interference. John has taken a strong stand against the project that Bob Hayes worked on and has had open conflict with other researchers, who often resent his openly pro-wolf stands.

Even his mentor created a situation that he has difficulty accepting. Pimlott's study of wolves in Algonquin Park included killing a third of the population to study the species' age structure. This incident did not diminish his respect for Pimlott. John says, "I think maybe he changed near the end of his life. The last dealing I had with him, he was dying of cancer and he phoned me up and asked that the memorial service end with the howl of a wolf. 'You pick a wolf howl to be played. I want it to be upbeat, not a mournful howl, one with pups in it.' One of the most emotional experiences of my life was at the memorial service when we played these wolf howls. Yet, ten years before he'd agreed to having wolves killed for research purposes."

John and other students of Pimlott went back to his journals looking for some Leopold-like quotes, but they weren't there. John describes him as "a hard-headed pragmatist." Like all mentors, Pimlott created a base from which the student must determine his or her own direction. "I now look upon myself as playing a different, yet complementary role," John says with a mix of pride and defiance. "Divorced from any government affiliations, my role as educator is to try new bounds of thinking on the public. That's not hard, because I have strong emotional feelings toward the wolf, so I'm trying those new bounds out."

He states that Canada must have large carnivore areas to preserve species like the wolf, grizzly, polar bear, cougar, and wolverine. The world often sees Canada as a land of endless resources, just as was once thought about the United States' own wilderness frontier.

His latest conflict is with the Ontario Ministry of Natural Resources over the status of wolves in Algonquin. John's position is consistent with that of Monte Hummel of the World Wildlife Fund Canada, who funded John's study of wolf mortality. The study indicates that the average mortality rate for wolves is extraordinarily high because they must follow their prey outside the park boundary and current regulations do not provide them with the protection they need. The park responds to the allegations by saying that "merely proving or showing exactly how some of these animals died doesn't prove anything," and they add that the study by Theberge is misplaced at this time. John will not back off and feels eventually the result will be a better policy.

In our continent's history we have celebrated people who have spoken out. From Rachel Carson to Henry David Thoreau, we have had respect for those brave enough to take a stand. Wise decisions are made on the basis of data and discussion. The accuracy and detail of someone's data are not a reflection of that person's ability to make decisions based on that data. It is important that the wolf biologists are tested from without and within. It is important that all knowledge pass through the crucible of criticism and that education remain a bastion of critical thinking. This is not to say that John Theberge is always correct, but Canada contains this continent's last great wilderness frontier, and the wildlife decisions that Canada makes will have consequences for the entire planet.

Wolves of the American Rockies

WHILE AMERICANS OFTEN talk about the rugged mountains of the West and marvel at the seeming invulnerability of the country's western ranges, it is also a fact that all wolves, of all subspecies, were eliminated in the Rocky Mountains, Sierras, and Cascades from the Canadian border to Mexico. Fortunately for the wolf, the Canadian West still held a reservoir of animals that was sufficient to provide emigration to the south. Now it is up to the United States to allow these populations to become established.

Wolves have been found in both Washington state and Idaho. The populations are small and vulnerable, and their ability to survive will depend on human attitudes and acceptance. Wolves and human hunters compete for the same prey; livestock competes with natural prey for territory and range. How tolerant we will be is an unanswered question.

In Montana, Robert Ream decided that he would investigate reports of wolves that he was receiving from ranchers along the Rocky Mountains. Of course, not all of the reports were accurate, but by scientifically plotting the most likely sightings, Bob found a territorial pattern, and, eventually, wolves immigrating into the United States from Canada were trapped and radio collared.

One of today's most prominent controversies related to the wolf is in Yellowstone National Park. In 1968, David Mech wrote about the need to reintroduce the wolf to Yellowstone. In 1972, Nat Reed, then park director, brought Mech in to set up a study to see if there were any wolves in the park, and researcher John Weaver confirmed that there were none. This opened up the question as to whether the wolf should be part of the park's ecosystem.

The reintroduction of wolves to Yellowstone is not a matter of economics or of biology, but of attitudes. The prey species are there, and without the fire that took place in 1988, Yellowstone might not have had the food supply to maintain its ungulate populations. What the elk herds, pronghorns, and others need is a predator that can help maintain natural relationships within the Yellowstone ecosystem. Without a predator, we have the potential for a major disaster if anything affects the food supply. Wolf biology in Yellowstone has now become wolf politics. How are ranchers to be appeased and compensated for predation damage? The livestock industry is demanding that if the wolves are put into the park, that they be collared in such a way that they can be instantly recovered. This technology exists, but wolves living under such restraints would hardly constitute a wild wolf population.

The drama will be played out in many human arenas before the experiment can be tested and evaluated on the mountain meadows where it belongs — unless the wolves move in naturally and eliminate the debate. There is some evidence that this might be happening, though not fast enough to eliminate the need for intervention. Until then, the best comparison for possible impact of wolf populations in Yellowstone is the study from Alaska's Denali National Park. Both parks are large, surrounded by wild lands, and include numerous ungulates, as well as grizzly bears and coyotes. In addition, both are highly visited. The key points from the Denali study are that the wolf does not limit the prey populations in Denali; the public is not endangered by the wolf; the public considers a wolf sighting as a positive experience; and wolves have demonstrated an ability to reproduce in areas of human tourism if their den sites are not directly impacted.

> *Wolf biology in Yellowstone has now become wolf politics*

Perhaps the question is best summed up in the following paragraphs from William Penn Mott, Jr., in his 1988 director's report entitled "Bringing Back the Wolf."

Ultimately, the question that keeps coming to my mind is: why not bring the wolf back to Yellowstone? I realize that my aggressive stance on this issue has created some controversy, but I don't take a stand on any issue based on the kind of reactions I expect to receive. Actually, when considering my position on wolf restoration, I find myself faced, time and again, with no other possible alternative. What other position could I take as Director of the National Park Service?

I ask this not in defense of my decision, but as an acknowledgment of my role—our role—as stewards of the national park system. If we don't accept this responsibility as stewards of the Yellowstone ecosystem, who else will? Furthermore, if we fail to accept the challenge at Yellowstone, what does this say about our ability to face challenges throughout the park system? And what does it say about our ability to be stewards of this system into the next century? It's a big responsibility, one too important to abdicate and one that we must continue to carry out, not only with flexibility—when flexibility is needed—but also with strong commitment and determination in keeping with the mission of the Service.

Throughout the mountain West, the wolf had been considered extirpated until the discovery of wolves immigrating into the Glacier National Park region. Since then, wolf reintroduction in Yellowstone has dominated the discussions and the press, but equally important are the wolves that have recolonized Idaho and their impact on that state. Now the question of reintroduction is complicated by the emigration of wolves from Canada. Even in the state of Washington there are now naturally occurring wolves that have reintroduced themselves.

In the Greater Yellowstone ecosystem, wolves have now been filmed, accidentally shot, and genetically investigated. The questions about reintroduction are complicated by the possible impact on naturally occurring packs and bring up another question about the corridors the wolves follow through the mountains from Canada. If we want to see natural immigration, we need to have more than a population with excess animals and a location with sufficient prey and area. We also need safe routes for the migrants to follow, connecting corridors that link safe havens. The questions, the answers, and the research will be complex for a long time.

Robert Ream

We met Bob Ream at the Capitol in Helena, Montana. He is a professor, a wolf researcher, and a state senator. Like so many of the wolf researchers we met, he is a complex individual who adds to the variety of backgrounds and approaches that helps all of us decipher the wolf's complex life.

From 1966 to 1969, Bob worked in Minnesota's Boundary Waters Canoe Area Wilderness with the North Central Experiment Station. He spent five to six months working out of the Kawishiwi Field Lab at Ely. His boss was Bud Heinselman, the researcher who unlocked the fire history of the canoe country. Bob met David Mech through a mutual friend. Bob and his partner were working on plant community sampling, and he had the additional responsibility of coordinating wildlife studies in the Boundary Waters. David had just begun his work in the Superior National Forest and he taught Bob the art of wolf howling.

Bob recalls, "I remember one time in particular. We were off the beaten path. I was taking some people on a 'show-me' trip—Forest Service people and a guy from the university. There were about six or seven [people] that came and howled, and a pack answered from quite a long distance off to the north. We waited about fifteen to twenty minutes and called again, and apparently a single wolf that split off from the pack came down to investigate. He answered from only a half mile [.8 km] away. We [howled] about three more times and he kept coming, until the last time I howled, he was less than one hundred yards [91 m] away. It was pitch black and we couldn't see a thing. We were camped on this narrow arm of the lake, and there was this channel fifty yards [45 m] wide, with a ridge going up to another ridge. The last time we howled, he answered right from the top of that ridge. Then you could hear him run down the hill. . . . He splashed into the water and then got out. We heard him pacing back and forth (the leaves were rustling) along the shore and a couple of times he would go into the water. Finally he just wandered off."

By 1968, Dave's studies had moved to the Kawishiwi Station and his field work in the Superior National Forest was just starting. Bob was with Dave when the first wolf was trapped and collared. Ream says, "Dave was pretty excited. He wanted to do everything right. . . . He had a trapper named Bob Himes working for him in finding the wolf. Bob was a pretty old guy who lived up near International Falls. We went out checking trap lines for two weeks right around Thanksgiving. . . . Finally we caught the first wolf right after Thanksgiving in 1968." The next spring, Bob accepted a job at the University of Montana. He had done his Ph.D. in the Wasatch Mountains of Utah in botany, with a minor in zoology.

"When I first came out here I asked people about wolves," Bob reflects. "The mammologist at the university showed me some specimens in the museum at the 'U.' One was taken in 1954. There were two others from '64 and '68 from around the south and the east side of the Bob Marshall Wilderness [in Montana]. Those were the only hard evidence we had that they had been there. There was a question mark in people's minds as to whether or not there were still some left. Dave came out and visited (we'd become good friends) in the summer of '73 and we did some backpacking in the Swan Range. . . . He stopped in to look at a skull that a taxidermist had, and based on our discussions, I started . . . the Wolf Ecology Project at the university."

This project, started in 1973, paid big dividends from a modest start. Bob says, "Initially our goal was to check out reports and to search areas for any evidence of wolves. It was the proverbial needle in a hay stack. But what I did, right off the bat that summer, was to send out several hundred letters to agency people, like Forest Service district rangers, Fish and Game Department biologists, trappers (we got a list of all the registered trappers), and outfitters. This was just a form letter asking them to forward any reports of wolves. I had a report form along with it to describe whether it was howling, whether or not it was a visual of tracks and that kind of thing. We started that fall. I think it was through Dave's efforts that the Northern Rocky Mountain wolf subspecies was added to the endangered species list. In 1978, they removed all of the subspecies from the endangered species list and instead the gray wolf species was listed as endangered in the entire lower 48, except for Minnesota, where it is threatened.

That's how it is at the present time."

The research was "opportunistic." Whenever they could scrounge up some money the researchers would move. The money was used for vehicles. Various students volunteered to go out and check on reports. They howled, looked for tracks, and documented anything they could find. From 1972–78, they collected data and analyzed reports. The incident reports concentrated on the east side of the Rockies all the way to Canada, from the Bob Marshalls through Glacier National Park. There was also a concentration on the North Fork of the Flathead River on the west side of Glacier. It was difficult to sort out all the varied data. They tried to eliminate the most obvious bad reports, but over a five- to six-year period there were four hundred reports to sort through.

In 1978, they got a three-year grant from Washington, D.C., to check out what Bob felt were the most significant possibilities. In the winter of 1978, a Blackfoot Indian trapper caught a wolf near the Canadian border, but still in Montana. That was a confirmation. Through January and February, Bob had two biologists working on the Rocky Mountain front near East Glacier. They battled winds and blizzards and had little to show for their efforts. On the North Fork of the Flathead, on the western boundary of Glacier Park, a grizzly bear researcher called. He said that he had seen tracks of several wolves during the winter, so Bob sent a biologist with one of Mech's trappers up to the area in March. In April 1979, they caught their first wolf, an eighty-pound (36-kg) female, and put a radio collar on her. They tracked her for two years and never found another wolf in the area.

Bob knew the history of Canadian wolves. He knew from various conversations that the wolf population would advance and then be held back by rabies or a predator control effort. They fluctuated up and down, but each up cycle meant a possible escapee for Montana.

The trapper thought the wolf was an older female, but her radio gave out in the fall of 1980, so they lost track of her. About the same time another wolf with a larger track showed up in the same area. One of the feet had only three toes, so tracks were easy to confirm. Then in the winter of 1982, Three Toes was joined by another wolf. They didn't know if it was the same wolf they had collared, but they did know it was a female. The pair mated and produced a litter just north of the border.

Diane Boyd was a graduate student who started her thesis work with the lone female, as well as with the coyotes in the area. Bob was now so convinced that there were wolves that he worked to develop a joint grant for Idaho and Montana. In persuading the states to put up the money, he guaranteed 10 percent from the university. He was confident, but had things gone wrong, he knew the 10 percent might come from his salary. The result was the Diane Boyd and Mike Fairchild project.

"I think the most significant thing in my whole experience was in 1985," he says with well-deserved pride. "Diane and Mike had been working out in the field and they had heard the Magic Pack [a pack that had crossed over from Canada] howl several times, but I had never heard them. Since we didn't have a radio on them, it wasn't easy to find out where they were. In 1985 I was here [in the capitol] for the legislative session. We go for forty-five days and then there's the transmittal deadline. It's really intense the last week or two, because you have to have all the House bills transmitted over to the Senate, and the Senate has to have all their bills transferred to the House. We take a four-day break and my wife, Beth, was out in San Francisco finishing up a film, so I had no reason to go home. I went straight up to the North Fork.

"A couple of volunteers had found a fresh kill and had tracked the pack, so we decided we would go up early the next morning and see if the wolves were near the kill. There was a spot you could stop, on skis, three to four hundred yards [275–365 m] away and see the kill. We had to snowmobile about fifteen miles [24 km] or so. It was twenty below zero [-28°C]. Diane pulled me behind the snowmobile on a long rope. I was on skis and had to stop several times to thaw out.

"We stopped the snowmobiles about a mile [1.6 km] back, skied in, and snuck up over the hill. We saw a coyote on the kill and a bunch of ravens and a bald eagle. We watched for twenty to thirty minutes I suppose, and I said, 'Let's try howling to see if they are around here somewhere.' I did a howl first and we heard this weird noise that we decided later was a wolf that started to howl and then just stopped all of a sudden, like the others had told him to shut up or something. We weren't even sure if it was a wolf. An elk sometimes makes a barking noise, and it was almost like that. It was just a short burst and [then it] stopped."

Bob continues, "We waited a little while and were puzzled. 'What the hell was that?' I said. 'Well, I think it might have been a wolf. Let's try howling together.' So Mike and Diane and I all joined in on a group howl. We no sooner finished, than the whole pack started answering us. They were only two hundred or so yards [182 m] away, off in the woods to the north. That was the first time in fifteen years or so that I had heard any, and the first I had heard out West. I was really moved. There were tears coming down my cheek. I gave Diane and Mike a big hug."

The pieces were coming together. Then the grizzly bear researcher caught a lactating female wolf in a grizzly leg-hold snare. It was the first of the Magic Pack. Montana research now had a base to work from. In the spring of 1986, the first documented litter in more than fifty years was found in a spruce forest, within twenty-five to thirty feet (7.6–9.1 m) of a meadow with a creek flowing through. Several den holes were dug into the side of a hill, with some of them interconnected.

Bob was on the Recovery Plan Team for Glacier and Yellowstone national parks, the Bob Marshall Wilderness, and Idaho. "When that Recovery Plan came out, the shit hit the fan. Primarily because of the idea of reintroduction in Yellowstone. That's what everybody focused on," Bob says with frustration in his voice. "We knew this was going to happen. In fact, I was one of the people on the Recovery Team who voted against reintroduction into Yellowstone at this time, because I knew it was going to raise red flags left and right. I felt like the whole Recovery Program might have been jeopardized with the administration that was in Washington.

People see a real difference between natural recovery and reintroduction

"People see a real difference between natural recovery and reintroduction. Natural recovery is an act of God, but reintroduction is an act of the big bureaucracy in Washington and they don't want to have any part of it. It wasn't that I was against reintroduction. My argument was that we have them coming back in Glacier, let's give that a chance for five or ten years. What the hell is the big rush? They have been gone for a hundred years. Give it another five years before we bounce this public.

"By a close vote, I mean it was a one-vote margin. . . . The Recovery Team was only advisory and made recommendations. The Fish and Wildlife Service issued the final plan and it was their decision . . . , partly with political pressure from conservation groups, to go ahead and push for reintroduction. I still think that it would have been better if we [had] held off. Recovery plans are supposed to be updated every five years. I think it would have been better to wait one cycle."

Bob's personal path began in Wisconsin, on a small farm outside Milwaukee, and included time at the University of Wisconsin at Madison. Between Madison and Utah, he also spent time studying at the university in Denver and at the University of Minnesota.

Even today, he is torn between the West and the Midwest, but his roots are deep in the Montana soil. At the University of Montana, he has tried to condense his teaching into two quarters to leave one quarter for research. The Montana Legislature meets every other year for just ninety days, and he has been part of it since 1982. These are ninety intense days, but all of Bob's work has been intense. Working with the wolf insures that there will be some controversy to deal with, but the satisfactions have made the controversy worthwhile.

While other researchers were studying established wolf populations, Bob was on the ground floor of a new and spectacular event. He got to see the beginning of a new population. As a result we now understand the immigrations into Idaho and Washington, and we can apply the same process to areas like Michigan, where wolves are now immigrating. The science of wildlife management for self-introduced species is limited, and this study is the baseline for many future decisions. Perhaps the lesson is a subtle one—if enough people are calling wolf, maybe there really is one.

Diane Boyd

We don't find it hard to believe that people can be fascinated by wolves and desire to observe them for extended periods of time. Should we be surprised to learn that some wolves appear to be interested in studying us?

Diane Boyd has had dozens of occasions when wolves have come by her house, stopped, and looked intently in her direction. The first time was in November 1983. She was writing a letter one morning when she heard a wolf howling. When she went to the door and cracked it open, she saw a big gray wolf standing on the riverbank across from her house. She managed to get photographs of the animal to prove the moment happened. The same wolf hung around off and on for almost two months. Diane has two very large neutered male dogs, and this wolf made them look small. From previous experience with wolves and dogs, she was concerned her dogs not be made meals of, so she kept them inside as much as possible. Eventually they got out.

The two dogs came charging out of the house and the wolf stood his ground. The dogs knew that this was not another dog and kept their distance. The wolf kept coming back anyway and playfully tried to lure them out into the field by crouching down on his front paws and swinging his big long tail back and forth.

Diane learned that the wolf was a male when it urinated on the bushes just as the dogs were doing. There never were any bad interactions. The same wolf was seen in the border area by several people, and he eventually traveled up and down the valley. He seemed to be quite unafraid of people.

On another occasion Diane went to the outhouse, since there is no indoor plumbing or electricity in her home, and as she walked she looked into a nearby meadow and saw what she thought was a very light-colored coyote. "I went back to the house and got my binoculars and looked and realized, 'My gosh, it's a real large, light-colored wolf,'" she says. "I got pretty excited because the very first female wolf we ever radio collared and studied on the project was #8550, who gave birth to the first wolf litter that we actually followed. Her radio had failed a year before.

"She was the only wolf that we had seen with this light color phase, so I kept watching her coming closer and closer and wondering if it was her, and she just kept walking toward my house. Pretty soon I could see the radio collar. I ran and snuck between the buildings so she wouldn't see me, and woke my partner. We got the receiving gear out and listened. There was no radio signal. We kept looking at her and pretty soon she got about twenty-five yards [23 m] away and stopped. She stood and just looked at my house. Then she turned around and walked back into the woods and disappeared. I can't help but wonder the things she was thinking. Like, 'Yeah, I'm still around but I'm smarter than you.'"

Diane expresses a sincere excitement and amazement over these unexpected encounters with wolves. They are a rare bonus in a researcher's life. Most researchers will tell you that though they love their jobs, there's not much glamour to them. The work can involve long hours under harsh conditions. Diane is one of a very few women in the field of predator studies. Names like Jane Goodall and Diane Fossey stand out in wildlife research, but very few women choose large carnivores as study subjects.

For Diane Boyd, life in the remote areas of Montana suits her fine. Growing up in the suburbs of Minneapolis, she was labeled a tomboy and still carries that description with her. Her interest in nature was sparked by a nearby marsh. "We used to wander through the muck," she recalls. "Once they put the interstate in, it sort of slowed us down. It was all fenced. We found a sewer system and used to crawl through the pipes and go under the highway. Before we discovered the sewer systems, we found a hole in the fence," she adds with a smile. "My parents never knew this. We'd get under the fence and watch the traffic and run across the interstate en masse. This whole crew of little kids with short legs."

In one junior high class the students had to choose a career and research it. Diane thought she wanted to be a veterinarian. When she was nineteen, she worked for a vet for a year, but spaying dogs and neutering cats for a lifetime just didn't live up to her dreams. She started college in pre-veterinary medicine but soon switched to wildlife management. Four years later she had her degree from the University of Minnesota.

During her breaks in college, and afterward, she did voluntary field work for Dave Mech in Ely, Minnesota. Then in 1978 she worked in Alaska on Prince William Sound, monitoring the sea mammals and bird colonies. The purpose of the study was to establish baseline data in case there ever was an oil spill. One of their assignments was to select a port that a leaking tanker could be towed into. With some sarcasm in her voice, she tells us, "They wanted us to choose a port [where an oil spill] would have the least impact on the wildlife of the area. It was like going around looking for an area you could destroy. It was a terrible thing to have to do."

About this time, Diane applied for graduate school. The University of Alaska contacted her and wanted her to study glaucous winged gulls. She decided that "after having worked with them in Alaska, and having been puked on and pooped on enough times by these aggressive gulls, I didn't want anything to do with it—although I did want to work in Alaska. I had written them a predator study and sent it in with my application."

She also applied to the University of Montana in Missoula but was turned down. Then, at the end of the summer, she got a letter saying they had funding, and one wolf collared—was she still interested? Remembering that momentous event she says, "So I got accepted in a last-minute rush. I finished up my trapping season in Minnesota, and drove right out to Montana and started."

Bob Ream was Diane's degree advisor at the time, and she still remembers their first meeting with embarrassment. "Bob had worked with Dave [Mech] up in Ely and he was really into wolves. He'd been dedicatedly collecting all this research information for years. I wanted to make a really good impression on him. I called his office when I was getting close to Missoula, and he gave me directions to his house. He told me it wouldn't be locked and to make myself at home. So I wander into his house, and there's nobody there. I was exhausted after having driven all the way, and I just sacked out on his couch. It was the kind of nap where you sleep really hard for two hours and your face gets all crinkled and your eyes are all puffy. I didn't even hear him come in the house, until he walks over and says, 'Hello.' 'Oh, hi. Glad to meet you.' Great first impression."

In the beginning of the study there was only one wolf collared—female #114. She was caught in April. "We followed her for sixteen months and then her radio failed," Diane says. "She was always alone, even traveling alone during the breeding season. After her radio failed we continued to follow the tracks of a single female wolf through the snow the following winter in the same territory. We saw no other sign of wolves anywhere in the area, except for her. There had been rumored to be a black wolf in '78 and '79, but we never saw evidence of it."

When Diane finished her master's thesis, the funding ended also. By this time she was totally captivated by her surroundings and didn't want to leave, so she stayed on and cut firewood, sold oil paintings, did whatever she could to stay in the area. She also volunteered her time and services to continue following the wolves. In the spring of

1982, a litter of seven pups was born. These turned out to be the first wolves born in the area in about fifty years. Diane saw the mother only once and she was gray, so it may have been the one that was first collared, #114, but they're not sure. The father was a black, three-toed wolf. Unfortunately he was caught in a grizzly bear snare and died.

That left the female to raise the pups alone. Diane was not optimistic about their chances for survival. "But, by gosh, by fall we were still seeing seven pups. It was amazing. I was finding their scats and collecting them, and they were almost all berries, which had me worried. I thought certainly these wolves aren't going to make it on berries. But they all made it into the fall. They seemed to be doing quite well, and they looked pretty healthy. I was really surprised, with just the mother to feed them."

Since 1979 Diane has made her home in this remote region of Montana, in the northwest corner of Glacier National Park. She lives in a very small and simple place called Moose City, actually an old homestead ranch. The nearest town is Polebridge, which is about twenty-five miles (40 km) away. Generally there are two people and one dog living in Moose City. The hay field is their runway. "We mow it once in the summer," she says, "when the grass is so long that the propeller can't get off the ground. I thought when I moved here to do my two-year study that I would probably get used to living here, and that was twelve years ago."

In the town of Polebridge there is a bar, a gas station, and an eighty-year-old mercantile. They don't usually shop for their groceries there, because a can of juice can cost as much as $2.00. The pay phone is set inside a wooden barrel on an outside wall of the mercantile. Chuckling, Diane says, "You call somebody and they say, 'God, it sounds like you're talking in a barrel,' and you say, 'I am.'" Wintertime residence runs to five people, two dogs, and two cats. In the summer the population booms with twenty to thirty residents.

Diane's most recent research work got going in the fall of 1984, when they received more funding from the Park Service, U.S. Fish and Wildlife Service, and the Forest Service. The study area is focused in the northwest corner of Glacier Park. According to Diane, "The terrain is very different from Minnesota and it results in some real interesting wolf behavior. We have a large valley bottom, from five to ten kilometers [3–6 mi], one river, about fifty to one hundred feet [15–30 m] wide, surrounded by mountain peaks. This mountain range goes on for twenty to thirty miles [32–48 km]. You have these big corridors of travel where the ungulates and wolves live in the wintertime. They're about two kilometers [1.24 mi] wide and fifty kilometers [31 mi] long. That's a limiting factor, I think, on the population."

A young male wolf, #841, was the first caught on the project. It may have been the same wolf that Diane had seen across from her house and interacting with her dogs. In May of 1985, they caught #8550, a nearly white female wolf. She had seven black pups and other pack members to support and helped bring food into the pack. This group was called the Magic Pack. They all survived their first year.

In 1986, #8550 had the first litter recorded in Glacier National Park since about 1910 or 1920. She gave birth to five gray pups. By the fall there were only three left. The researchers were never able to find out what happened to the other two. In January 1987, during the spring denning season, #8550 split off from the pack and formed the Sage Creek Pack. Meanwhile, another lone wolf picked up a mate and formed a pack in the next drainage, and all of a sudden there were twenty-five wolves. In 1988, the second pack, named the Wigwam Pack, had another litter, the Sage Creek Pack also had a litter, and a third pack formed. This one was called the Headwaters Pack, and consisted of two male wolves and a third wolf of smaller stature, most likely a female.

When #8550 split off, she basically carved off the northern half of the range. The researchers wondered how the packs were going to divide the territory when winter arrived, because all the game comes down to the same river corridor. As it turned out, one pack defended that entire territory. The Sage Creek Pack was severely reduced by British Columbia hunters, since Canada has a hunting season on wolves. Of the five pups born, four were killed and one of the adults was killed, so by October all that remained of the original pack of ten was the alpha female and one pup. Two of the other adults had dispersed.

In following the wolves and their division of territories, Diane and her fellow researchers have observed long-distance travel, as well as more typical dispersal patterns. The first wolf that they caught, #841, had a huge home range. He was a loner and covered an area of 2,300 square miles (5,980 km²). He crossed the Continental Divide twice in the middle of the winter. Diane is folksy and possesses a ready laugh, which she shares as readily as her stories. "In 1987 he picked up his mate, and he immediately, like all good married people, settled down, put some roots in, and stayed within the Wigwam drainage. His home range site is about 150 square miles [390 km²]. That's what having kids does." Diane continues, "One of the pups we radio collared left Glacier Park in December and we lost track of her. She left the area so fast we couldn't keep up with her. The following July she was shot up near British Columbia. In that seven months she'd gone 550 miles [885 km]."

The research has turned up a territorial behavior not found in lone wolves in Minnesota—scent marking. In Minnesota, single or dispersing wolves try to minimize scent marking and try to keep their presence unknown. The wolves in Diane's study area seem to want to advertise their presence. Dave Mech suspects that "if they smell the sign and scent posts of the wolves as they pass through a saturated population, they're inhibited from marking, but then they get into an area with no marks and that turns them on to mark. If there are other marks, they don't want to be known. But if they get into a new area, they do want to be known."

Like Peter Clarkson, Diane has also recorded animals "visiting" with other packs. She describes one incident. "She was an interesting animal in that she was a member of both the Camas Pack and the Sage Creek Pack. When we'd fly, I'd see her with the Camas Pack. She'd be down on the ground and there'd be puppies climbing on her and chewing on her. Two weeks later I'd fly and she'd be up with the Sage Creek Pack. Same behavior." Unfortunately this animal crossed about a mile (1.6 km) over the Canadian line during hunting season and was shot. This destroyed Diane's hopes of seeing where the wolf would spend the winter months.

In order to observe these sorts of behaviors and movements, the researchers must capture the wolves and radio collar them. This is a very time-consuming and rugged business, but just one aspect of the year-round work. "One of my main roles for the project is as a trapper," Diane says, enjoying the reaction she gets from people who don't expect a woman to be involved in that sort of activity. "Once the animal goes down [with a hypodermic], we attach ear tags, radio collar, and draw blood samples, and we check the animal over to make sure it's in good shape. If we catch one that's really small, we just ear tag it, make sure it's okay, and let it go.

"When you get pups in the fall, about five months of age, they weigh sixty pounds [27 kg]. Their skulls are not full sized. What you have to do to make the radio collar fit is you take the collar and, based on the sex and the size of the animal, you fasten the collar to an adult neck circumference and then you take foam rubber and line the collar and wrap it all up with duct tape and just push it over his snout and ears. The worst thing that can happen is that it falls off."

Diane relishes her work and is animated as she tells what she does. "We examine the foot that was in the trap to make sure it's not damaged. Then we give them an antibiotic, and after everything is done we just back off and watch and wait for them to come up. Once we get the collar on, we radio track from the ground, and because there's one road that runs up and down the length of the valley, we can usually track the main pack in Glacier Park along the length of this road. Ground tracking does present problems at certain times of the year when the roads are pretty impassable.

Sometimes the wolves play jokes on us

"Two of the packs are more remote and we have to fly to locate them. We attach an antenna to each wing. It's like stereo. Where the signal is strong, you turn and follow it till you get over the animal and then you can circle over the pack. When we do fly, we land in the hay meadow. In the winter we put skis on the plane. . . . We fly and ground track and get radio locations. Then we ski along their tracks and travel on the wolf route and map the important routes and corridors, and collect kills and look at their food habits. There are times when you wish you were on snowshoes. The forests are pretty thick with a lot of lodgepole pine.

"Sometimes the wolves play jokes on us." She laughs and continues, "One morning, we skied up the river and the wolves were about four miles [6.5 km] north and we were going up to track them. When we came back, a pack of twelve wolves had come down the river on top of our ski tracks, in broad daylight.

"I really enjoy the winter work. Finding the kills is definitely the highlight. That's the area I'm particularly interested in. I found the skull of one elk calf about a mile and a quarter [2 km] away from a kill. An elk calf skull is not little and it doesn't have any nutritional value. I think the wolf started taking it as a trinket. If there are remains, we collect what is useful and analyze them. If the marrow looks like strawberry jelly, then you know the animal was in very bad condition and probably would have been dead in a few days. When an animal is in the process of starvation it uses up the fat supplies within its own body and, in effect, starts digesting itself. One of the last things it absorbs is the fat of the marrow. Normal marrow looks like what you buy in your grocery stores—the butcher bones with light, creamy fat."

Diane's humor, the twinkle in her eye, and her ability to tell a good tale take nothing away from her skills as a researcher and scientist. She continues, "We also look for abnormalities. Oftentimes it's real difficult to determine what happened. When we're looking at deer kills, it's hard to get information, especially in a mild winter when the wolves eat the hooves, the skull, everything. I have found kills where there's not even blood. You know there's been a kill—you fly over and see it from the plane—and you wait till they abandon it, and you go in two days later and there's nothing there. Nothing. It's just incredible!

"When you find elk you generally find a little more evidence. When you find moose, they generally don't crack the real large leg bones or the skull. We collect the pelvis of the animals—if they're available—to determine the sex. We collect the jaws if possible, pull an incisor in the front, and send it in for aging. By counting the rings, just like on a tree, they can determine the exact age of the animal. We also collect all the wolf scat we find. We wash them out, sterilize them, and go through the hairs. A laboratory analyzes what species are present. What you find in the scat record and what you find in the actual kill can be different. As a result, whitetail deer are probably under-estimated, because oftentimes there's nothing left of the kill to find."

Collecting scats is just part of the routine in research work, but it can lead to some interesting comments by friends and associates. "One year I was in Canada and we were collecting scat." She laughs at the memory. "I have some friends who hunt that area and one came up to me later and said, 'You know you sure have got these wolves well trained.' I said, 'What do you mean?' and he said, 'I was down in the river bottom the other day and, by gosh, I found a scat in a baggie.'"

After the winter work comes spring breakup. This presents other challenges, like the river ice thawing while you're on the other side. There may still be two feet (.6 m) of snow on the ground, so tracking is a possibility, but it will be ten degrees (-12° C) in the morning and fifty-five degrees (13° C) in the afternoon. This causes the wolves to lie down during the afternoon hours—when their legs punch through the snow—and wait till nighttime to travel. Then the researchers take snowcats out and the crust is so frozen that they can barely see the scratch marks made by the edge of the skis. Obviously this makes finding tracks very difficult. The researchers try to locate the wolves with radio telemetry in hopes of determining where they are going to den, which usually happens in April.

After the wolves leave the dens, typically in late August, Diane and her coworkers go in to measure and map them. The dens are generally fourteen feet (4.2 m) deep, and oftentimes have a T in them. There'll be one area of the den that's a little larger, like a chamber three feet (.9 m) across, but most of it is about sixteen to eighteen inches (40.6–45.7 cm) wide. The dens are clean, with no bad odors in them. Around the wolf den and the rendezvous sites the researchers find lots of scat, which is collected for analysis.

During the summer, Diane will trap and collar wolves and then radio track them, but she rarely goes in to any kills during the summer months. Occasionally, if they spot wolves from the air on a kill they will go in, but the problem is that there are grizzly bears roaming the landscape and they frequently take over wolf kills.

"One time, I was flying and saw the Headwaters Pack and they had a kill, and I was really excited. The wolves were about fifty feet [15.2 m] from the edge of the trees, wide out in the open, and I thought, 'Wow! Look at those wolves,' and the pilot said, 'Yeah, but look at the bear!' Here was this monstrously huge grizzly bear . . . hanging over the carcass." Demonstrating, she says, "We circled down lower and as we got lower the bear started jumping up and down on its front feet and threatening the plane. We went back up. Unfortunately, I didn't have my camera. It would have made a most incredible picture.

We find oftentimes that the grizzly bears are benefiting from the presence of the wolves. One might hypothesize . . . that the presence of the bears makes the wolves kill more frequently. We do find the bears taking the kill away long before [the wolves] are finished."

Diane sets a target for the number of wolves in a particular pack that she wants to capture and will work until she has reached the desired number. Then she pulls everything out and moves to another area. When fall arrives, trapping is curtailed because Canada has a big-game season that starts on September 10, so fall work involves mostly radio tracking. By Thanksgiving in the U.S., snow generally has fallen and they can begin snow tracking. First they radio locate the animals, and then they go into the area where the wolves were the day before. They do this by skiing in until they cut the wolf tracks, and then backtrack. Two people going in together head in opposite directions and start over the next day until they get as many continuous miles of track as possible. Winter tracking leads them to the kill sites.

Diane says, "They have a tremendously large prey base. We find they kill about 56 percent whitetail. The mule deer that come down onto the winter range are on private land and the wolves pretty well stay out of that and stay in the park. They get about 35 percent elk, 8 percent moose, and the other 1 percent is made up of beaver, small rodents, and assorted strange things, like grouse, ravens, and skunk. We found where they had killed a skunk, but they ate only the front half."

While deer make up the main prey base for the wolves, they are not necessarily easy to catch. "If you've ever had a chance to work with deer, [you know] they can be pretty formidable," Diane tells us. "You try to pin them down and they can really kick hard. I think about the wolves, every time they go to eat, they have to catch it in their face.

"There's a big . . . distinction that people like to make about wolves taking the sick, the old, and the weak. I prefer to say that they take the vulnerable. A hunter may say a bull moose is in his prime, but in reality that bull may be past his prime. He's a trophy animal, and he'll defend his herd, but while he's out fighting and harassing and getting beat up, the little bulls sneak in and do most of the breeding," she says, smiling at the irony.

"What happens is these guys really work their brains out during the fall, and they go into winter in very poor shape. They can lose two hundred pounds [90.8 kg] of their body weight just from rutting. They cease eating for a month. Deer do the same thing. They rut very hard. They go into winter in poor shape, and the older males of both the deer and elk are oftentimes the ones that the wolves get. Snow conditions can make a big, healthy animal vulnerable too, not the condition of the animal itself. Generally the most vulnerable animals are the young of the year. We find in both deer and elk about 50 percent of all animals killed are the young of the year."

Just as the lives of the deer and elk are difficult, so sometimes is the life of the researcher. One has to be prepared for unexpected hardships and learn to make the best of the situation. Diane recalls an experience with one young intern who found out about the drawbacks of field work.

One night, out in the middle of nowhere, the truck they were driving started to have problems. They tried unsuccessfully to get it going, but finally around midnight they realized they were stuck for the night. The temperature dropped to twenty degrees (- 6° C) and with no sleeping bags and just lightweight clothing they resorted to Diane's bag of laundry. They wrapped towels around their heads and put their hands into socks. Diane was not overly worried or bothered about the situation and fell asleep in about twenty minutes while sitting behind the steering wheel. Before she fell asleep she could hear the young man muttering, "This is hell man, this is hell." Diane slept till dawn, but the intern, who was skinny as a rail, never slept at all.

In many unpleasant but unusual situations, in retrospect one can find humor in them. Diane is able to laugh now about an encounter with a grizzly bear one summer. She happened to have the same young intern with her at the time. Curt was twenty-one years old, fresh out of college, very enthusiastic and excited about the work, and he had never seen a grizzly bear in his life. He had been working with Diane for about two weeks when they caught a wolf in a trap. This was a wolf she'd caught the previous fall as a pup. They went through the processing and checked the collar fit and then carried it into the shade deeper in the forest to wait for the anesthesia to wear off.

The wolf was thirty to forty feet (9–12 m) away from the researchers. As they were putting away the capture kit and supplies, they heard some twigs snap in the underbrush. They both looked up, but saw nothing. Suddenly Curt yelled, "There's a bear!" Diane looked up and sure enough, "There was this BIG grizzly bear and it was coming towards us," she says. "The first time we saw it, it was about forty to fifty yards [36–45 m] away. We were in real thick lodgepole forest, not on the road." The bear stopped and looked at them. Diane told Curt to go and get his jeep, which was out on the road. He started off running, then stopped, and walked the rest of the way. The jeep had a ripped canvas roof, windows that were all ripped out, and a bad carburetor.

Meanwhile Diane is back in the woods and the bear starts moving in her direction. Diane hypothesizes about the reason. "I think when you catch a wolf, like if your dog's ever been hit by a car, they exude a real strong musk, [a] fearful smell. There's some trauma and a little blood in the capture. The bear was smelling this because it certainly knew we were there. It could see us and hear us and smell us."

The bear kept advancing and Diane, lacking any weapons, stood up and picked up her red clipboard and slapped it a few times. The bear stopped, stood up on its hind legs, and looked about fifteen feet (4.5 m) tall to Diane. Curt still had not returned and Diane continued to yell at the bear. Finally she heard the sound of the jeep engine struggling to start. When it finally caught, the bear, which was about thirty yards (27 m) away, turned around and ran. Curt backed the jeep up at about thirty miles (48 km) per hour to a section of the road that was near Diane, but they were still separated by a good expanse of forest. Curt couldn't get out of the jeep because if he did the engine would die and he feared he wouldn't be able to get it started again. While he was trying to keep the engine running, the bear returned and started toward Diane once again.

Diane remembered the wolf and recalls her thoughts and actions. "[I thought,] I put it in this position. It can't respond, it can't get up. So I start going kind of toward the wolf and the bear is coming towards us, and I'm clapping and yelling and carrying on, and it's getting closer and closer. It stands up again, drops back down, and comes in to about fifteen yards [13.5 m]."

Diane started yelling to Curt to honk the horn. He finally heard her and laid on it. The bear turned and ran into the woods. Diane is not a big woman, but years of working in the bush have toughened her, and at this moment she had to call upon all her strength and courage as she recalls, "Without thinking, and it was nothing heroic, it was just a response like when you get in a car wreck and you just react, as soon as that bear turned, I ran over and picked this wolf up. They're pretty big, but I got it kind of around the ribs and I'm trying to drag it out, and when I do, it's being stimulated and it's starting to come up anyway, so it starts twitching and starts to swing around. I'm dragging it between my legs, waddling down the road and yelling for Curt."

She laughs as she remembers, "He was having a hard time trying to get out [of the jeep] with the [lousy] carburetor and finally he takes an ax and wedges it between the gas pedal and the seat and comes flying out of the car. His eyes were like saucers. I'm yelling, 'Curt, help me. Come here.' He finally comes running out and takes the wolf from me." The wolf by this time was more alert and trying to bite, so Diane grabbed it by the jowls around the ruff and held the face away from Curt, and they continued to walk and guide it toward the jeep.

The excitement doesn't end there. One of Diane's dogs was sitting in the front seat of the jeep, looking out the window. Diane opened the door and threw the wolf in. Immediately the dog was growling and the wolf was trying to grab the dog's feet. "I'm beating on the dog and trying to get the wolf in the car," she says. "We jump around the jeep and by now the wolf's rump is smashed right up against the stick shift, and its business end is beating on the dog and the dog's beating on it. We go down the road about thirty miles [48 km] an hour in first gear because we can't shift because the wolf is there.

"I don't know where the hell the bear was. I never looked back. We go down the road about two miles [3 km] and I say, 'Pull over here.' There's a little logging road, and we carried the wolf down the steep hill and placed it in a bunch of sphagnum under some spruce. It [was] nice and cool and shady. Then we walk back up on the top, sit down, and watch the wolf come up. Curt says, 'I'm working for a crazy lady.' I said, 'That's okay. It'll get better.' Anyway the wolf eventually got up and was fine, the bear was fine, and we were fine."

Just as Diane's parents never knew about her youthful escapades of crossing the freeway, she neglected to tell them about the bear encounter until a few years later when she was home visiting and some neighbors were over. Her parents yelped, "You what?" Diane's response was, "Oh, you know, just another day at the office."

John Weaver

Talking about Yellowstone National Park, where he conducted the research that confirmed the absence of the wolf, John says, "It's a great habitat for ungulates, but a principal predator is missing. To have a large population of ungulates without a predator is not natural. Its absence has ecological significance. It's not like you're missing a species of mouse. You're missing a primary component of the whole system."

From 1975 to 1977, John Weaver roamed the expanse of Yellowstone. He would spot tracks from an airplane, then ski or snowshoe to measure and identify the canid that made them. Unfortunately, the largest native canine was only a large coyote. John walked, howled, and set up time-lapse movie cameras. He checked old sites, historical data, and local stories. Twice he saw tracks that may have been wolves'; once he heard howls that might not have been coyotes'. The conclusion was easy to draw: There is no viable population of wolves living in the Yellowstone area.

John wrote, "Two options are available for wolf management in Yellowstone National Park: (1) do nothing; or (2) attempt to restore a viable wolf population by introduction. The former alternative has been employed since 1927 when wolf control ceased in the park. In the past fifty years, a viable population has not reestablished, and the wolf niche appears essentially vacant. Therefore, I recommend restoring this native predator by introducing wolves to Yellowstone."

> *To have a large population of ungulates without a predator is not natural*

John Weaver grew up in Texas, wanting to be a wildlife biologist. He migrated to Utah State University and then to Jackson Hole, Wyoming, where he did his master's work on coyotes. His study in Yellowstone was the result of good timing. In addition to being in the area when Dave Mech persuaded the National Park Service to do a survey to determine if there were wolves, his study of coyotes established him as a canid researcher. He spent twelve months, over a period of two years, in the field. Historic studies established that wolves were nearly gone by the mid-1930s. His research provided data for the wolf project. His devotion to the subject didn't end there, even though his studies moved on to other topics.

John's field experiences weren't all contained in his published work, as we were to find out. The following vignette demonstrates the unpredictability of field research. In John's words, "I was back in an area of Yellowstone that was closed off to overnight camping because of the grizzly bears. They had some reports of possible wolves back there, so I felt obligated to go back and do my thing. I went into this big open valley (it's called Hayden Valley, where the Craigheads concentrated their research) about eight or ten miles [13–16 km] and set up a camp on top of this little knoll. I was half a mile [1 km] from the nearest tree and broadcasting tape-recorded howls.

"It started to get dark, so I played the first set of howls, cut it off, and waited. A few seconds later I hear this 'Grrrrrrrrr' and my heart just comes down. I took a deep breath and waited a few minutes, then played another set of howls. Off on the left side about a hundred or so yards [90 m] away—'Grrrrrrrrr!' I waited about another twenty minutes, played another set of howls on the same ridge that I camped on, and not more than seventy-five to a hundred yards [67.5–90 m] away — 'Grrrrrrrrr.'

"I folded up and crawled inside my tent, got right in the geometric center of the tent, just lay there, and didn't move. All night [something kept] going back and forth by my tent— 'Grrrrrrrrr.' I'm just waiting any moment for a big hairy leg to come through the tent. I didn't shut my eyes once that night. It was in August, so it got daylight about 5:00 A.M. I unzipped my tent, looked around, stretched, but didn't see any bears. Then I noticed this bull buffalo standing about hundred yards [90 m] away. I didn't pay much attention to him. I walked around a little bit more and then I hear this 'Grrrrrrrrr!' and it's this buffalo!"

John shakes his head and continues, "I'm going, 'How can you even call yourself a wildlife biologist and lose a whole night's sleep because you don't even know what a bull bison sounds like?' I'm sittin' there kicking myself mentally and the next second, here comes a grizzly bear about fifteen yards [13.5 m] from me. I had camped on a pretty steep side and it was the first time he could see me. The wind was in my favor. He stood up and I stood up. It was a young bear, probably three or four year old. He just started running about fifty yards [45 m] downwind, stood up again, got my scent, and just started grazing. I wasn't in much shape to walk anyways, so I watched him for a while and finally after some further meditation decided get the hell out!"

Right after the Yellowstone project, John worked in Brazil on a jaguar study on the Bolivian border. He was working in one of the largest swamps in the world—an area ten times the size of Yellowstone. He became the first researcher to radio collar jaguar. In 1985 he took a Forest Service job as the national grizzly bear habitat coordinator. This project lasted three years, and during that time he lobbied to do wolf research in western Canada. Since western Canada represents the most logical source for Yellowstone wolves, John felt that we needed to know the animals at the source to understand how they might react to relocation. In 1990, he finally got his opportunity and moved his family to Jasper National Park in Alberta, where he got a job as a wolf researcher.

John reflects on his life of wildlife studies and his personal feelings about the Yellowstone issue. "You know we have an unparalleled opportunity in a place like Yellowstone (which is one of the largest remaining, almost intact ecosystems) to get the wolf back. We have a place that's 15 million acres [6 million hectares] of just wild land."

Bob Ream and John Weaver disagree over the process for wolf recovery. Bob advocates natural reintroduction, and John says, "That's a point of severe disagreement between Bob and myself. I think that the biological evidence from other places in North America and what we know about dispersal [indicate that] the sort of critical mass of dispersal that is necessary to get recolonization [is not here]. You have to have more than a few [wolves] every once in a while. You have to have a steady stream, and that stream falls off the farther [the] distance from the [primary] population. The majority judgment of the Recovery Team was that the likelihood of natural recolonization was so remote that it wasn't a viable recovery strategy.

"The Recovery Plan by law is supposed to be the biological blueprint for the species. If you don't maintain the integrity of that document, then you are just going to slip the rest of the way. My feeling is that I had an obligation as a Recovery Team member to make this the best biological blueprint. Then, if in a different arena people wanted to make the judgment that it wasn't politically timely to pursue it now, that was fine, but we had to keep those arenas distinct.

If something isn't right ecologically and you have a national policy that calls for recovery of endangered species, and if you have a land management policy for restoring things, then it is a worthy goal to pursue with everything you've got."

John emphasizes his stand when he says, "The West, unlike Canada and maybe Minnesota, has been without wolves, so even the older people don't have much of a memory of what it is to have wolves. There's a fear of the unknown, the uncertainty. So as advocates, if you will, of recovery, all we can do is point to other places where people more or less tolerate wolves."

John's work points out the complexity of bringing science to the public. It is too easy to draw examples from word of mouth, to make statements that reflect unrelated circumstances. The issues of wolf recovery have been drawn together in Yellowstone—it is the magnifying glass for future wolf issues. The conflicts between scientists are understandable, just as the conflicts between wolf advocates and wolf haters are inevitable. The significance of John's role is the fact that the ultimate decisions related to all wildlife issues must address all the issues and finally come back to the species itself. If we are committed to saving our biological diversity, we can't afford to debate good versus bad. Sometimes the issues transcend science itself and the real factor is the ethics of the decision in the light of our growing understanding of global ecology and complexity.

6

The Red Wolf

IT IS POSSIBLE THAT the red wolf existed in North America before the gray wolf and the coyotes. Fossils 750,000 years old indicate that the red wolf may be a close relative to a primitive ancestor of the North American canids. Recent advancements in biochemistry and the investigation of genetic structure have led to questions and controversy over the true genetic nature of red wolves. Some scientists feel the red wolf originated from a hybrid between a gray wolf and a coyote. Others feel that the fossil record, and the facts that existing red wolves bear unique traits and continue to breed to type, prove their distinction from the gray wolf and coyote.

William Bartram, an eighteenth-century naturalist and author of *Travels,* first described and identified the red wolf in 1791. Then, as the settlement of the country expanded, they began to suffer the same fate as all other predator species. Their historic range covered the southeastern portion of the United States, reaching as far west as Texas and north to Illinois. They seemed to prefer warm, moist, and densely vegetated habitat, although they were also present in pine forests, bottom land hardwood forest, coastal prairies, and marshes. Destruction of forests and coastal marsh habitat, as well as widespread persecution and predator control activities, brought them close to extinction. In 1980, they were declared biologically extinct in the wild.

From 1973 to 1980, forty animals were captured, but only seventeen of these were considered purebred red wolves. They became the founding group for a captive breeding program with the hopes of saving the species and, possibly, reintroducing animals into areas of their historic range that offer some degree of protection and adequate resources for their survival.

It is believed that the minimum viable population for the red wolf, given the number of founder animals and reproductive limitations, is five hundred animals—two hundred in captivity and three hundred in the wild. Currently, there are fewer than one hundred animals in both wild and captive situations. The goal of the captive breeding program was to get wolves back into the wild as quickly as possible, because in small, captive populations a species begins to lose genetic variability, and the evolutionary process stops.

During the 1970s and '80s captive breeding programs across the United States brought the number of red wolves up. By 1978 the first trial release occurred on Bull's Island in South Carolina. Initially there was some public antagonism toward the reintroduction programs, but Fish and Wildlife biologists were quick to point out that the wolf tends to feed mostly on small mammals, not deer. The red wolves released initially would be highly managed, allowing recovery personnel to monitor the animals with radio collars and retrieve any that strayed out of the prescribed release area. Any animals that threatened human safety or property would be returned to captivity.

Currently, red wolves have been placed on Bull's Island in South Carolina, Horn Island in Mississippi, and St. Vincent Island in Florida for natural propagation. The offspring have been released at a primary site in Alligator River National Wildlife Refuge in North Carolina, and in 1991 they became the stock for an experimental release in Great Smoky Mountains National Park on the Tennessee and North Carolina border. The animals in the Smoky Mountains were put out, studied, and then recaptured.

The "experiment" in the national park has the potential to be a great success story, but there are many challenges to be faced. Smoky Mountains has the highest visitor use of all our national parks, its half-million acres (200,000 hectares) have only a few roads accessing a small fraction of the park, and poor weather and extreme topography make ground and aerial telemetry difficult. There is also a good-sized coyote population in existence, and a private livestock concession with three hundred cattle located nearby.

The fact that the park has such high visitation rates can also work in the wolf's favor, since the National Park Service can apply its extensive interpretive programs to the education of the general public on the wolf and the reintroduction program. This in turn may build a larger base of support for the species reintroduction to the wild.

The longest-running success story for the red wolf is in Alligator River National Wildlife Refuge. In 1984, 118,000 acres (47,200 hectares) of land was donated by the Prudential Insurance Company, through the assistance of The Nature Conservancy. This brought about the creation of a wildlife refuge offering critical wetland habitat, not only for the red wolf, but for migrating waterfowl as well. Directly adjacent to the refuge is a Department of Defense bombing range, of which 19,000 acres (7,600 hectares) are being managed for conservation, in effect expanding the habitat for the red wolf to over 135,000 acres (54,000 hectares).

This land of nonriverine swamp forests, pocosins (a thick evergreen understory of shrubs), and brackish and freshwater marshes is within the historic range of the red wolf. It is situated on a peninsula that is sparsely settled. There are only two paved roads, and approximately fifteen hundred people live in four small communities near the refuge. There are no coyotes or feral dogs in the area. All these factors were ideal for a reintroduction program and rare in the southeastern U.S. In the fall of 1987, when the first red wolves were released into the refuge, it was the beginning of the first project in conservation history designed to restore a species that was extinct in the wild.

Mike Phillips

Mike Phillips, a biologist with the Fish and Wildlife Service, first heard about the Alligator River project in 1984 while at a meeting in Sydney, Australia. He was working at the time on a Rotary International–funded project on dingoes.

Mike is a gregarious researcher who punctuates his conversations with bursts of laughter, color, and the local vernacular. Telling how his research career began he says, "I was walking around . . . the Life Sciences building [at the University of Alaska] and I saw this ad for Fellowships offered by Rotary International. I went into my advisor's office, and I said in jest, 'Well, hell, maybe they'll send me to Australia to study dingoes.' I'd always wanted to study dingoes.

"A couple weeks passed and I was sitting at my desk and I said, 'What the hell, I ought to at least call the guy.' So I called him and we immediately hit it off. I went and spoke to [the Fairbanks Rotary Club] and they liked me enough to sponsor me for the local competition, which went in my favor. So they sent me to Seattle for the regional competition, and that went in my favor. So they sent me to Australia to study dingoes," Mike says with a laugh.

Mike is decisive, probably a little impulsive, and definitely action oriented. "I got married right before I went, and my wife and I left for Australia in December of 1983 and returned December of 1984. My wife, Tanya, helped me do the field work. We did about eight months of radio tracking dingoes and red foxes in the southeastern corner of Australia. It was just tremendous."

The experience gave him more background working with canids and capture techniques and "just a general feel for what working in the woods is all about. Every day you're out something is registering, whether you recognize it immediately or not. It went a long way toward helping me gain experience in organizing a project, dealing with logistics."

When that project ended Mike returned to Alaska, where he accepted a job with the Fish and Wildlife Service doing grizzly bear studies in the Arctic National Wildlife Refuge. He finished his master's degree at the University of Alaska and he also began lobbying for the job with the Alligator River National Wildlife Refuge. He already had a working relationship established with Dave Mech, having worked for him in Ely, Minnesota, for ten months and later at the Carlos Avery National Wildlife Refuge in Minnesota.

In February 1986, Mike met Warren Parker, the head of the red wolf project. This led to a phone call in March with a job offer Mike couldn't refuse. He moved from Alaska to North Carolina in July, and his wife followed in September. She had had a job with the Fish and Wildlife Service in Alaska doing research in arctic fisheries, which she thoroughly enjoyed. Luckily there was an opening with the Division of Marine Fisheries in North Carolina monitoring the commercial fishermen. She got the job, and together both scientists found satisfaction and challenge in their new careers.

Mike Phillips has blond, boyish good looks and the demeanor of a modern Andy Griffith. His background fits that image pretty well too. "I was born in Charleston, Illinois, and lived in Boise, Idaho, and Seattle, Washington, until I was about five, and then we moved to Champagne, Illinois. That's where I grew up. Up until I was about twenty or twenty-one, all I really wanted to do was play professional baseball. My father was with youth baseball and we started as seven-year-olds with farm league, and then it was Little League, and then it was Little League All Star, then it was Babe Ruth, and Babe Ruth All Star, American Legion, American Legion All Star. [Dad] had three sons, about a year split, and we just kept moving up to the various levels and ultimately concluded with the semi-pro league in central Illinois. My dad played pro ball for the Phillies, but I quickly realized that there's a lot of people who can make money playing baseball, but there's very few people who can make a living at it."

Mike discusses the interests and options that he balanced in deciding on a career. "I had always been really interested in biology and I've always liked dogs. As a junior in college, I reckoned I'd better get my act together academically. I started studying harder and spending more time at school and less time playing ball and drinking beer. I got in with some real good people and went to one of my profs, who's a very well-known ecologist—name is Jim Carr. He was my advisor, and I started asking him a number of questions about graduate school, and he really got pissed off at me and said, 'Look, I'm not going to do your leg work. You go out and you find what interests you. You get the names of the schools and then you come back and we talk.' That was tremendous advice."

Reflecting on that time in his life, Mike says, "I had come across Dave [Mech's] book about six months prior to that and found out there was a visiting professor at the University of Illinois that had Dave as one of his Ph.D. advisors, so I took his [Roger Powell's] course and got to know Roger real well. I wrote Dave and expressed an interest in working with him. He wrote back—it was just a form letter, which is understandable—and said, 'I appreciate your interest, but if you want to work with canids, I recommend you work with coyotes or foxes. There's a lot more opportunities there.'

"So I got together with the fur biologist with the Illinois Department of Conservation and we did a study of winter food habits of coyotes in southeastern Illinois. We looked at the stomach contents of about 250–300 coyotes and wrote a paper for the state journal. Then I wrote

Dave back about a year later and said, 'I'm getting closer to graduating. I've done the coyote work,' and as luck would have it, Dave had a position opening the same month I was graduating. He had a need, I was available, and he brought me on."

Even though Mike left baseball behind as a career, that background has had some unexpected and important benefits for his work with the wolves and the Alligator River National Wildlife Refuge. "When I was playing hardball I thought softball was for fellas who couldn't play hardball, and I was a real snob about it, but I've played now for three summers here . . . I've met a lot of nice people and it's a way that they've had a chance to meet me. With the wolf project being so visible, that's extremely important because the ball team is comprised of mostly local hunters that have proven to be very important allies."

Mike's relations with the locals and the hunting community is very important for several reasons. "We told people going into this project that deer would probably not be a big food item. My comment was, 'We don't know that. Food-habit literature concerning red wolves is scant at best. To make those kinds of statements, I think we're just opening ourselves to criticism, because three years from now, we may find deer are an important food item and the folks are going to be saying, 'Look you told us wolves weren't going to eat deer. We supported the program thinking it wouldn't affect our success in terms of hunting.'

"There's a lot of deer hunters in the Southeast. I think we need to hit these people with information up front that says wolves are going to eat some deer, and try to convince them that that's not such a bad thing. Even if they have to expend a little more effort to get their one deer, it's worth that for having wolves out."

While it is believed that the red wolves will be feeding initially and primarily on marsh rabbits, muskrats, mice, nutria, and an occasional raccoon, they will take deer if presented with the opportunity. Mike reports, "We have had wolves kill deer. We had an animal that choked on a raccoon kidney [and he] was clearly a deer killer, him and his mate. We found half a dozen kills from those guys, and we weren't really even looking. I'm confident that the three big food items in Alligator River once there's a population established will be deer, rabbit, and raccoon. The order and importance may shift from one year to the next, or one season to the next, but whitetail deer are going to be an extremely important food for red wolves in the Southeast.

"I've proposed a hypothesis that as time passes in Alligator River, or for any closed system as the area becomes saturated with wolves, a young wolf is faced with a very difficult decision concerning dispersal." Mike's train of thought is momentarily interrupted as he considers the future. "Hell, there's no place to go. Puppies born in the refuge now have a pretty wide open slate to draw on, because all the spots aren't taken yet and there's pretty good spots to go to establish your own home range and do your own thing. That's a good strategy to maximize your genetic fitness, but ten years from now, all of the spots are likely to be occupied, so a pup may conclude, 'Well, I might as well stay home, and help rear some siblings and pass on my genes that way, and perhaps boot out one of my parents at the appropriate time.'"

Mike develops this hypothesis for the expanding population. "If they are as territorial as we believe they will be, then of course there's strength in numbers from a social standpoint, too. To support that kind of sociality—the increase in group size—I think they're going to have to start working whitetail deer even more to support the group. Two or three animals can feed on one at a time. That just doesn't happen with a rabbit or raccoon. The deer here are relatively small, most are going seventy to eighty pounds (31.5–36 kg).

"I think group size in wolves is more a function of sociality than prey size. In effect, for gray wolves there's strength in numbers. The bigger the group, the greater your chances of surviving interpack conflicts. To support that big group, you've got to have a pretty big food item." Remembering one significant discovery, Mike says, "We had a male. I had him from the air at 6:30 A.M. We checked him about 2:30 P.M. and in that eight-hour time period, he killed a deer and ate 60 percent of it, all by himself. . . . Sign in the road indicated that he simply jumped that deer, got close enough, ran it down, knocked it down, and killed it."

On another occasion, Mike was able to find a kill site and interpret the interaction. "I was flying one morning and I saw one female at an intersection. We were interested in some fresh stool samples to float for parasites, so I came back on the ground and I went to where I'd seen her. I picked up the turd, and I was trying to figure out if she went back to where she was keeping the puppy. I continued to track her, and she had moved a considerable distance back to the pup. I figured, 'What the hell, I'll just stay out the rest of the day.'

"I went back to the spot where I found her from the air. I got about a mile [1.6 km] away and I started listening and I couldn't hear [the pup]. They usually don't go anywhere in the day. You find them at 6:00 A.M. and they're going to be there at 6:00 P.M. He wasn't around, so I started driving the road and on my way back out, I saw a big scat in the middle of the road. I stopped, and as I was picking it up, I noticed a couple little pieces of deer hair and then a little piece of rumen. I thought, 'What the hell's going on?'"

Sharing his thoughts, Mike continues, "I started poking around, and clearly what had happened was that the wolves had been traveling south on the road and had jumped about three deer. The deer had continued south—you could see where the wolves had been chasing them—and they cut off to the west. The wolves slammed on the brakes, cut off to the west, and knocked one of the deer down about ten feet [3 m] in the woods."

As Mike relates these stories he is animated and immersed in the memories. "The kill site at this point was nothing but the rumen and a big hair mat. We found a couple chips of bone. What makes it all fascinating was obviously I'd seen the female traveling away from the kill site. I had located them both at the kill site that morning. Both adults were gone by noon—six hours later. They had been seen the day before south of the kill site, traveling north, so during a twenty-four-hour period, they had seen those deer, killed one, consumed all of it, and left."

Expressing some amazement, Mike says, "Let's assume conservatively that [the] deer weighed fifty pounds [22.5 kg]. In a matter of twenty-four hours both of those animals consumed approximately twenty-five pounds [11.3 kg] of food, and they found it within themselves to get back to the puppy and do what adult wolves do."

Captive wolves in the program are fed dog food and then shifted to a meat diet prior to release. The spacing of feedings is also altered as they near release from a regular schedule to the more natural system of gorging and then going for several days without food. If after the wolves have been released the researchers suspect that they are not finding food—most notably by the lack of scats—they offer supplemental feeding, usually in the form of a deer carcass.

Mike tells us about one case that occurred early in the project. "Female #205 was released with male #184 in the eastern part of the refuge. They did real well but #184 was an animal that was seen some seventy times along the highway. He just wouldn't get off the doggone road. They went ahead and produced a litter of puppies. Number 184 was bringing food back to #205, that was rather obvious, and then he got hit by a vehicle on May 29. By the eleventh of June, #205 had decided to move. Obviously she wasn't able to make a go of it near the acclimation pen without #184 bringing food back.

"I got a call on a Saturday morning. Some guy said, 'I just saw a wolf and a pup on the highway.' I thought, 'Yeah, right, but I better go check it out,' and sure enough, I pulled up right near where she was. She had a radio collar on, so I was able to get right on top of her. I heard one puppy whining after her. As soon as it got dark, she came back out on the highway and she walked that puppy up the highway. Apparently she felt she had no choice. She had to get to the farm. The puppy was only about six weeks old, so he wasn't really capable of moving through the heavy vegetation . . . she was going to use that highway, come hell or high water. We had our truck, so we stopped traffic. We just escorted them right up the highway. As soon as she got to the first dirt road, she cut off to the west and they disappeared.

It's going to be a very intensively managed population until it's gone

"She walked the pup [#351] up to the farm, and recognizing that she was still lactating and had to do this all on her own having never done it before, we decided to start feeding her once again. . . . about two pounds [.9 kg] of food per day. It helped insure that #351 made it to a reasonable age.

"It's tough for us to truly understand what's going on out there, if a wolf is feeding itself well . . . or not," Mike admits. "Our approach at this point . . . is to err on the side of the wolf, by giving him too much food. The only problem with a long-term supplemental feeding program is that association between humans and food, or vehicles and food."

Aware of the controversy it might cause, Mike says, "I don't have any moral problem with feeding these animals. It doesn't matter. It's going to be a very intensively managed population until it's gone.

You're not going to have wolves in Alligator River without an intensive management program and at times that program will call for putting out food. That's the best we can offer the red wolves in the twentieth century. It's a strange kind of freedom, but it's better than a pen."

There is very little known about the red wolf's natural ways. Few studies were done of the species before it became extinct in the wild, so the researchers at Alligator River are learning as they go and speculating about the animal's future behavior. In a few short years they have already gained some significant insights. In 1991, a female wolf was found dead, apparently killed by another wolf over territory or competition for the only available male in that area.

Mike reflects on current information. "The verdict is not in yet on just how it will behave and what ecological role it will ultimately fill. We don't know a great deal about the home range requirements. . . . The preliminary work here at Alligator River suggests that they will be territorial, which of course will mean they'll need even more country. It seems that they will be relatively violent with one another in territorial disputes. We've clearly had two fights—one almost resulted in the death of the wolf. He was so badly injured, I can't understand why they didn't kill him outright."

Relating the incident, Mike goes on, "We had two acclimation pens within about a mile [1.6 km] of each other. We released four wolves at the same time and soon after release we picked up sign in the road that indicated the four wolves had interacted." One of the wolves was seen in the pen of one of the other wolves, sleeping in their dog box. The researchers concluded that he had displaced them, but then the other wolves came back and attacked him. In the meantime, the other female kept leaving the refuge. The researchers speculate that she was keying in on the territorial behavior of the other wolves. The researchers caught her once and brought her back and released her, and she left again. They brought her back again and put her in a pen. At some point the two free-ranging wolves returned, got into a fight with her through the pen, and almost tore her front leg off.

The researchers have found that the wolves will scent mark frequently when other wolves are in the area. "When there weren't other wolves out, you didn't see any scent marks," Mike says. "As soon as wolves come in here, boy you pick up huge scent marks, big scratches, four- to five-inch [10- to 12.5-cm] circles, just all tore up."

Because of these territorial encounters, Mike Phillips sees "immediate implications to . . . management and how we conduct these release programs. We don't want to release wolves on top of one another anymore." He believes that based on the body size of red wolves, a pair will need a territory of twenty to thirty square miles (52–78 km²) of good country. The goal is to have a minimum of 220 wolves at three or more sites. Mike adds, "We don't want to hang our hat on just one or two study areas for fear that some strange event would wipe us out."

The wolves that are released now come from captive stock, or preferably from animals born in the wild at one of the propagation release sites. Mike tells us, "The Bull's Island program objective is simply to produce puppies that are slightly wilder and go through a more rigorous selection process than . . . the captive-born pups. . . . They will be used to inject more wildness into the captive population. Some of the animals are going to exhibit behaviors that are life threatening upon release, behaviors they've developed after spending years in captivity. Highways can be a real problem. For the most part, they have done reasonably well, but we've seen some problems with certain individuals. We've had animals freeze up in the woods on us. I had to throw a stick at one wolf to get it to move. We've had animals approach trackers."

Working with the animals in the pens, the researchers try to have as little contact with them as possible so that the wolves maintain their natural shyness around people. The pens are set up in a heavily forested area, and there are large pieces of plywood covering the sides that face the trail and work areas. Mike Phillips lives twenty minutes away from the refuge, but he'd prefer to live closer, even on the site. He says, "I miss a lot. I don't experience the weather that the wolves experience. I think you develop a better feel for what's going on if you're . . . living out there."

At Sandy Ridge (the name of the captive breeding site at Alligator River), the plan is to develop a captive population that consists of a variety of red wolves of different ages and different reproductive histories, "so we can respond to damn near any strange event in the wild. We're trying to diversify our program to complement the free-ranging population," Mike says.

"We interact with the animals here in a very different way than

Rolf [Peterson] . . . on Isle Royale or Dave [Mech] in Ely. It's just the nature of the program." Emphasizing these differences, Mike says, "We feel very strongly at this point that puppies shouldn't be released before about ten weeks of age, so that we have the opportunity to do a number of things to them. We hit them with a dewormer at four and eight weeks. We hit them with vaccinations at six and nine weeks, and by eight to nine weeks they're old enough to handle an implanted radio, which we feel is very important because it gives us an opportunity to work with the puppies before they're old enough to wear a collar. So you're looking at ten to twelve weeks before they can be released, if you want the pups to have about two weeks in a pen to convalesce after the surgery."

Once the animals are released into the refuge, a lot of the work involves the collection of scats. Mike describes this important but less than glamorous task. "I would guess if you have a dozen to twenty wolves in Alligator River, with any kind of crew at all that can spend time on the ground, you should be able to collect six to eight hundred scats a year, conservatively. You're picking up fifty a month, ten a week. It gives you a pretty good feel for what's going on. When the wolves were first released the scats were either empty—they didn't seem to contain any hair or bones—or we weren't finding any. If you're not seeing any fecal material at all, you gotta start wondering."

The first nine animals that were released were implanted with radioactive disks that marked their excrement, so about 70 percent of the seven hundred scats collected can be traced to the wolf that deposited them. This allows the researchers to look at the transition that an individual wolf makes from dependency on humans for food to self-sufficiency. There are also records of where each scat was found. By combining this information with the telemetry records, it is possible to determine which wolf was where at a particular time, adding more data to the project.

Retrieving the animals if they wander off the refuge is another important part of the job. They sometimes wander south of the refuge into an agricultural area. Mike describes the procedure. "Currently, when a wolf leaves our land, we've no choice but to bring it back. Our approach . . . might be to wait and give it a week to see if it comes back on its own. We've shown pretty clearly that although you can effect short-term changes in wolf movements, they're going to damn well go where they please. You gotta believe they know more about what they need than we do, and if they want to go somewhere there's probably a pretty good reason for it."

Recognizing the importance of the techniques used to capture stray wolves, Mike says, "The public is, largely, judging our ability based on our recapture success. If we fail in those attempts, they're going to conclude that the project itself is a failure and they're not going to give us the benefit of the doubt."

Mike becomes animated as he relays a personal experience. "I always get a charge when we catch a wolf when we have to. Think about trying to catch an animal that's so capable of avoiding people. We've had some tremendous dart shots. One time, it was the thirty-first of January, Super Bowl Sunday, and I was all settled back. Chris [was] flying that morning and he came home and said the wolf is down by the farms, out in the middle of a corn field, way south of the refuge. So, Chris and I and Tanya got all the gear and went down there and we saw the wolf out in the field. We're driving around the field, keeping the wolf boxed in. We left Tanya with the vehicle to sort of act as our herder. Chris had a dart rifle and I had a dart pistol, and we worked up on the wolf. It chose to bed down in the ditch, probably hiding from me. I got real close to him and right as I saw him, he saw me and took off. I went ahead and shot and I just barely hit him in the elbow. The dart was just barely hanging from a flap of skin, but it was enough to get him to go down. We were able to bring him back and we didn't miss a minute of the Super Bowl. It was tremendous." Mike punctuates this story with his infectious laughter.

As that story demonstrates, the wolves don't always choose the best moments to wander or require intervention. Mike tells of another such incident on a Friday night. "We had been really working on these Bull's Island puppies, and I went and played racquetball. I was bagged, wanting to stay home. I was going to watch 'Dallas,' I had ordered a pizza, and I was just getting ready to get relaxed when Chris called and said one of the pups is on the highway. I said, 'There's no way that puppy's on the highway. I just located it six hours ago and he was well south of this road. He would have had to have traveled ten miles [16 km] during the heat of the day. Are you kidding me?' and he said, 'No.' We went on for five minutes and finally he got mad and said, 'Look, man, I'm telling you there's a wolf on the highway.

We're going to go out and check it out. I just wanted to find out where the other set of headphones was located.' I said I would come by and go with him. I just couldn't see them giving up their Friday night with me propping my feet up at home, drinking beer, and watching 'Dallas.' "

Working well with other staff at the refuge is a key to the success of the program. "I tell the guys on the project that I look for people that are independent thinkers, because I don't have all the answers. I look to those guys for ideas. It's not uncommon for us to make decisions based on group consensus. If they deviate from the plan that's not necessarily bad, so long as they can justify the deviation."

While building the pens is the hardest physical labor on the project, Mike finds the office work and data organizing to be much more overwhelming and personally challenging. He says, "The most tedious and the stuff that worries me more than anything else is the data management. . . . We've got a tremendous amount of computer work to do. You really don't start any analysis until the data are entered in a computer and the files have been proofed. I hate to divorce myself totally from the field. I mean it's not why I got in this work, and you lose touch if you don't come out. Your interpretation of the data starts to suffer because you haven't got that gut feeling about what in the world's going on."

Mike sees the intensive management of the red wolf as the wave of the future. "Clearly, one of the values I see for this program is that we are a preview for the future of wildlife biology around the world. I think that we've shown that captive stock can be used and can adjust to life in the wild. That wasn't known beforehand. We've also begun to scratch the surface at the kind of management program that's necessary for these restoration projects. The large mammals are going to become more and more endangered and, ultimately, I would be willing to bet that all the large mammal populations will exist in a megazoo-type setting, where you've got to concern yourself with the fate of the individual animals . . . and manage them on a daily, very intensive basis."

Even in such a tightly controlled environment, with lots of intense management, the wolves still face the hazards of dog-related diseases and other natural dangers and disasters. Hurricane Hugo hit Bull's Island and the adult male is believed to have died as a result of injury and stress from the storm. Four puppies survived the storm's fury, but earlier in the summer one pup and its mother were killed by an alligator.

At Alligator River, the wolves have navy jets occasionally roaring overhead on runs from the nearby bombing range. It sometimes startles them, but for the most part it's just another part of the environment that they ignore. The wolves in the pens are sometimes stimulated to howl by the noise of the jets, with the puppies usually initiating these howling sessions and the rest of the wolves joining in.

According to Mike, some wolves will probably get bitten by snakes and some snakes will be eaten by wolves, although determining their presence in scats is very difficult. He adds, "I don't think they'll be a real important food item, but this area is a herpetologist's dream — lots of snakes, lots of frogs, lots of turtles, and those will be food items for the wolves." The researchers have already encountered a number of cases where the wolves have uncovered yellow slider turtle nests and eaten the eggs.

While food items wouldn't normally be considered dangerous to the wolves, one animal did die from choking on a raccoon kidney. He had been killing deer and raccoons for fifteen months. According to Mike, "It was just a crazy accident." Another wolf, a female, died of a uterine infection after giving birth. This was a female who had produced two or three litters in the wild.

These are just some examples of the random, unpredictable events that can hit a project, and for Mike Phillips it highlights the fact that "you've got to tell the local and general public that these programs aren't going to be immediately successful in terms of seeing low mortality. Likely, you're looking at losing a lot of the initial animals to one cause or another. That isn't reason for undue concern, and it's no reason to cancel the program.

"One guy in the Red Wolf Recovery Team was talking about these unusual occurrences of death and he said if people were to radio track animals with the same degree of intensity and frequency that we do, likely some of these strange sources of mortality would be much more commonplace. He related a story of one of their bears that was hit and killed by lightning. Now how often is a black bear going to be killed by lightning? He also said they found a case where a raccoon had been killed by a limb that fell off a tree. It's tough to make a living in the woods. Nobody has really taken captive large carnivores, released them, and then tracked them over a long period of time to measure their success."

With pride, Mike states, "In some respects, given the timing and historical significance of this project, ten or fifteen years from now it could very easily turn into another long-term study of the wolf and how it makes a living, much the same way that Isle Royale and northeastern Minnesota have been."

Mike feels that "the production of two litters during the first breeding season is evidence that the program is tremendously successful." In 1991, three litters and possibly a fourth were produced by free-ranging red wolves. One of these was a second-generation wild breeding. "In addition," Mike says, "the Recovery Team is arguing that our ability to locate the wolves whenever there's a need is evidence of success."

As a means of maintaining the present success and improving the prospects for the future, the researchers are working on developing techniques to move genetic material from one population to another. As Mike explains, "Though Alligator River may only support a dozen wolves, we need to be drawing on genetic material from four hundred and we do that now by shifting animals from point A to B and using new genetic material. We're also looking at trying to refine techniques from embryo transplants and also the preservation of germ plasm—sperm, etc."

A program such as this is extremely expensive, estimated to cost around $7.5 million for five years. Currently funded by the federal government, the team is always searching for outside sources of funding. With a glint of humor in his eyes, Mike adds, "I'll probably put my suit on and shave, and get my hair cut and go to the businesses in the area and see if I can't get them to adopt red wolves. See if I can't get the local high school science teacher to take his science classes every year and have them adopt a wolf and have benefit car washes, or whatever. We'll try to make sure there's reasons for them to get involved."

Sometimes the challenge of it all seems impossible and Mike finds himself wondering about other approaches and careers. "You wonder, 'Is this the most effective route to follow? Would you be more effective as an influential businessman, making $2 million a year and taking 50 percent of your earnings and buying land?' . . . The money wouldn't be the motivating force for me. The motivating force would be, 'Could I be more effective?'"

But then he shakes his head and returns to the present. "The red wolf program in the Southeast should continue despite the fact that the wolf life form is well represented elsewhere. With a touch of pride in his voice, he concludes by saying, "The program has matured. We're doing more things now than anybody thought. We're the second-largest captive facility for red wolves in the world . . . the only real staging facility for red wolves in the world. I suspect in five years you'll probably always see at Sandy Ridge fifteen to twenty-five wolves in pens at various stages of acclimation, just getting geared up to adjust to life in the Southeast so they can contribute to the overall program to preserve the red wolf."

On September 30, 1992, the experiment to re-establish red wolves in Alligator River National Wildlife Refuge came to an end. Forty-two wolves had been released on fifteen occasions and North Carolina had thirty free-ranging wolves. Over the course of five years of study, twenty-two of the forty-two released animals died and seven were returned to captivity. Most important was the fact that at least twenty-two wolves had been born in the wild, and one of the eleven adults that produced offspring in the wild was born in the wild herself.

Mike Phillips sees this project as a precursor to the future when growing human development will mean highly managed populations of wild animals. It is to be hoped that we will never need to control all our populations in such a manipulative way, but if another species survival depends on captive breeding and individual monitoring, Mike has helped establish the parameters for success.

7

The Mexican Wolf

THE SMALLEST SUBSPECIES of wolf in North America once roamed the border states of Texas, Arizona, New Mexico, as well as most of Mexico along the central plateau south to Oaxaca. The climate was drier and sparser than in the other wolf ranges, and much warmer than in today's ranges. This area's severe climate makes harsh demands on all its ecological components. The natural balance is most easily disturbed in areas like this, where each species is surviving under duress.

As much as poisons, guns, and traps, the wolf's demise in the Southwest was due to the demand for marketable beef and the supplanting of natural grazing herds with cattle. The decline of deer, pronghorn, elk, bighorn, and bison led wolves to livestock and human conflict.

In 1977, Roy McBride, a U.S. Fish and Wildlife trapper and biologist, was commissioned to conduct a survey of the Mexican wolf. His assessment project located a small population just 230 miles (368 km) from Big Bend, Texas, and he found that a wolf may have been killed north of Big Bend in 1970. From 1977 to 1979, McBride live trapped four Mexican wolves—three males and one female—that formed the basis of the Mexican wolf captive breeding program. Since the 1979 survey, no wolf sightings have been confirmed in Mexico.

In 1982, the Mexican Wolf Recovery Team was created. For the next decade, the team would meet, talk, and search for a chance to move forward. In the meantime, Mexican team member Julio Carrera said, "I am very angry about what is happening with the Mexican wolves." He fears that as the original wolves die out, their wildness will disappear with them and new generations will be unfit for the wilds. Carrera wanted to see action taken immediately.

Peter Siminski

The Mexican wolf has not had field naturalists doing research on free-ranging packs. Until 1993, there were no funds and no organized field study. Now the effort to study Mexican wolves in the wild must begin by determining if they even exist. Our information base relies on historical data and captive wolves.

Peter Siminski works at the Sonoran Desert Museum of Tucson, Arizona, one of the original three breeding locations and the organization maintaining the stud books for the Mexican subspecies. The museum got its first Mexican wolf in the 1950s and has been one of the leaders in pushing for reestablishment in the wild. At the time of our discussion in 1989, the captive breeding program already had to combat the limitations of a small genetic reservoir. Only two of the founding group were still alive—a male and a nonproducing female. Peter was hoping to store semen from the male for future fertilization. Peter told us, "If we get one good breeding pair and they're producing a lot of pups, we don't want their genes swamping the rest of the population. That pair will have to be broken up."

The breeding program has a goal of one hundred wolves in zoos in preparation for reintroduction. To accomplish this, other zoos are being added to the original three of Tucson; Albuquerque, New Mexico; and St. Louis, Missouri. Peter is very aware of the problems facing Mexican wolf reintroduction and he shared his pragmatic view with us. "Ideally, you would want five hundred wolves, but you're not going to find enough room to hold five hundred wolves. Ideally, you would want fifty founding animals, but there aren't fifty animals to be taken for stock." The population at the end of 1991 consisted of forty-six wolves, including seven pups, in zoos and a few unconfirmed reports of wolves in the wilds of Mexico. The hope for the Mexican wolf depends on coordination between the state and federal governments of Mexico and the United States.

Breeding of wolves is complex because wolves are complex animals. Zoos are given approval for Mexican wolf breeding, but just because the zoo puts a male and female together does not mean that the pair will mate. Most of the time, introducing a male to females is routine, although on one occasion when the Sonoran Desert Museum put an old male in with four females in the nonbreeding season, the females just bullied him. Introducing females to other females is always more complicated. The Sonoran Desert Museum has found that pairs will breed if the other wolves are separated, but this still does not insure complete success. In 1991, only the Rio Grande Zoo of Albuquerque had successful litters. Nine pups were born and two died of canine parvo-virus. Six pairings in other locations were unsuccessful. In addition, as on Isle Royale in Minnesota, there are concerns over the genetic health of a limited population.

Wolves are intelligent and have long memories. Roy McBride, in his Mexican wolf report, tells of captive wolves remembering him as a source of food after an absence of many months. Peter Siminski says, "They are very keyed in to our keepers. We've had a student on top of our buildings watching one of the wolf pens. We have these little electric carts that drive up and down the grounds, and the wolves could tell before they were in sight which cart was which and when the keeper's cart was coming.

"The wolves know who's a keeper and who isn't. Our vet comes once a year to give shots or a physical examination, and all our wolves know when the vet is coming around. They howl and stomp because they think he's going to come in there. They are extremely observant, aware animals. We have one old male on exhibit who is completely blind and no one can tell. He knows when a keeper goes by or when the vet is standing around. He can't see him, but he can smell him."

Even after years of studying wolves, Peter is still awed by their complexity. "The thing that surprises me about wolves is their volatile nature. By that I mean they can be extremely loving to one another, but the next minute they can be extremely severe. Their sensory ability is something that I don't think humans fully understand or have an appreciation of." Drawing from years of personal anecdotes he adds, "Our former curator used to say, anytime you want to lock wolves up into a kennel, just us sitting in the building thinking about it will have the wolves out there thinking, 'Oh, they're going to be locking us up in the kennel today. Let's not go out there,' and the only way to do it was to just go out and do it and not think about it."

Another problem is the purity of the gene pool. Are all the Mexican wolves in zoos really the Mexican subspecies? There is a captive pack of wolves that is maintained in the United States but not used because of questions on lineage. The Sonoran Desert Museum maintains the stud book to protect the future, but it may be DNA research that ultimately provides the answers to subspecies' purity.

The folly of *Homo sapiens* seems to be reflected in this wolf. For generations, bias, ignorance, greed, and power bring an animal to the brink of extinction. Then we get a pang of conscience and spend more money trying to help the animal cling to existence than it would have cost to preserve it in the first place.

The captive breeding project presents a problem, but more serious is the need to reverse centuries of public prejudice, ignorance, and fear. There is a need for habitat protection, as well as wolf protection, but the fact remains that Mexico has a third-world economy that is not oriented to wildlife concerns. Mexican farmers, ranchers, and peasants are not used to regulations on hunting or trapping, and their war on predators was made twice as effective by the slaughter of prey species for food. There are very old Mexican laws that would protect the environment, but they are neither funded nor enforced. Now the Mexican wolf is a national priority, but no one knows the steps to take to make it a viable species again.

Maybe it is a statement in itself that the wolf's greatest hope for survival is to be released on a missile testing range

Even in the "environmentally enlightened" United States, there are major problems for Mexican wolf reintroduction. Texas rejected the project and passed a law in its state legislature to prohibit wolf reintroduction, even though Big Bend National Park might be a significant option. No sites had been identified in Arizona until 1993, and more studies are being done. In New Mexico, White Sands Missile Range was chosen for a release location, but was temporarily put aside as an option because the army did not want civilian researchers on site.

Debate and conflict dominate this battle, and politics more than biology will control the wolves' future. Maybe it is a statement in itself that the wolf's greatest hope for survival is to be released on a missile testing range.

Julio Carrera

In the world of wolf researchers, haters, and supporters there are many emotions. Seldom is anyone neutral about the wolf. The result is an ongoing conflict that often masks the real issues about the plight of the wolf. Julio Carrera of Mexico is a person of emotion and concern. He has served as a member of the International Wolf Committee and on the Mexican Wolf Recovery Team, but his concern extends far beyond the wolf, to environmental education and environmental issues in his own country.

A balding, mustachioed man, Julio's mild-mannered, kind demeanor belies the passion he brings to wolf meetings. As Mexico's former Director of National Parks he watched policies shift according to who was in power, he watched the rainforest in Vera Cruz fall to the saw, and he saw the wolf eliminated. His job required him to live in Mexico City, a city of more than twenty million people where air pollution permanently blocks out the blue sky.

Julio's appearance reflects his ranching background, and he appears most comfortable wearing a western-style shirt and bolo tie. His interest in wildlife began on his family's ranch in the state of Puebla. When they sold that ranch and bought another in Vera Cruz, he was introduced to the rainforest. "At that time the government wanted to produce more cattle and crops [by selling state land to farmers]," he says. His father was one of the people that the government sold the land to.

"I . . . arrived when most of the place was quite pristine. I was lucky enough to see jaguars and monkeys. It was just beautiful! That's why I got interested in nature. I decided to be a veterinarian and I studied in Mexico City. I didn't like the city, so I went to northern Mexico—Chihuahua—and did animal husbandry at the university. I was more interested in grazing cows, but I still had a love for the outdoors.

"My father was a hunter, and I hunted with him since I was very young. After I finished with university, I got involved with the wildlife aspects of the outdoors. . . . I was working for the National Institute for Animal Science Research . . . in ranch management and the wildlife aspects of the range, like predation of coyotes and wolves. At that time, even grizzly bear were found."

While the rainforest was being eradicated in the south of Mexico, the Mexican wolf was being killed by the poison 1080 throughout its natural range. The poison has been banned since 1973, but enforcement is very difficult. The last confirmed sighting of a wolf in Mexico was in 1984, but Julio is not convinced that there are no more wolves in the wild. He is frustrated with the efforts today and that is reflected in his voice as he says, "I'm not closed to the idea that perhaps there is no viable population left in Mexico. But I'm not convinced of that. Americans say, 'Well, let's forget about the Mexican wolf, because there is no one left,' but I do not believe them, and they are not producing information that can be checked so I can be convinced. On the other hand, I still keep telling everybody, there are still some Mexican wolves left in the wild, but I am not able to show reliable information that proves my point."

Julio's concern is that we don't become so enamored with captive breeding that we stop efforts to protect whatever wolves might still exist in the wild. Reproduction in the natural state is still the best chance of saving the species, but because of the glamour of captive breeding and the fact that the captive breeding program is mostly a U.S. project, Julio believes there is less money available for work in Mexico. Because Mexico is large and wolves would be in remote areas, Julio feels the researchers must be Mexicans, who understand the culture, the language, and the animal.

The Mexican people do not have the stereotypical big, bad wolf. "Our tales are imported ones," Julio says. "That is perhaps because the wolf disappeared around the cities too long ago, so they didn't develop any tales, and the people in the rural areas are too busy working to invent tales." Tales of the Aztecs are not well documented and the wolf is not prevalent in their artwork, unless there is a confusion with the coyote. Julio feels that the Indians who lived near the wolf were respectful of the animal. Even the cowboys with their love-hate relationship respected the animal.

Julio faces the same challenges from ranchers as the people proposing reintroduction in Yellowstone. With a combination of hope and desperation, he tells us, "It's the same all around the world where wolves and cattle mix. Cattlemen don't want to hear about the wolf, but this new collar is very promising to me. I was talking to some people in the state of Chihuahua—cattlemen that I have known since long ago. I know they don't like anything like grizzlies or wolves around, and they told me that if I could promise them, and show them, that I could take again the wolf, or even kill them, then they will let me put some wolves on their ranches." (The collar that Julio refers to is the radio-controlled capture collar that L. David Mech has developed in Minnesota.)

Wolf research in Mexico is the same combination of talking and tracking that dominates other parts of the wolf world. The trouble with tracking is adapting it to a landscape that does not accept tracks easily. There are no planes, helicopters, snow, or muddy areas to help. While studies are needed now, research methods must be developed simultaneously. Julio looks to the techniques Bob Ream used to determine wolf presence in Montana; he feels that similar work could be done in Mexico.

With a chuckle at the memory, Julio says, "Most of the time we have nothing to do with the wolf. It is always interesting to work with the young students. We developed a technique to know if howling was a wolf or not and it was a quite simple one. Most of the students working with me didn't know about the wolf, especially in the wild, and they kept asking me, 'How can I be sure if the howling is a wolf or something else?' We usually told them, 'You will know.' Usually we slept in a tent and when we heard a howl, if the student crawled into his sleeping bag we knew it was a wolf."

Historic records of wolves in Mexico don't indicate large packs but rather two to four animals moving together and then dispersing. One of the things that drives Julio is the memory of actually observing a Mexican wolf. He recalls the incident. "It was quite something to remember. I saw it in Chihuahua. I was driving along with one of my students. We were looking for the owner of a ranch to ask for permission to go onto his land. Very near the ranch house we saw the wolf. It was very funny because my student, he is very good in the field. He is a hunter since very young. Nevertheless when he saw the wolf he told me, 'Look at the coyote.' I told him that is not a coyote and he told me, 'Oh no, it's not a coyote. It's a shepherd dog, a German shepherd dog.' It was too big to be a coyote, so he thought it was a shepherd dog. This was about nine years ago."

The efforts of the U.S.-Mexican Wolf Team have not pleased Julio. He has seen political appointments of people who were not sympathetic to the wolf, and he has seen funding disappear. He complains, "The Mexican Wolf Program was funded with $33,000 for the survey of the wild populations and the money never arrived. It was an agreement between the two countries. Unfortunately, the same thing happens in Mexico. The people changed so much and the politics got so upset that they didn't follow up what happened with that agreement."

Julio's frustration becomes apparent as he talks about the captive breeding program, "They did nothing for the wild ones," and about the researchers, "I do not understand the so-called research people who do nothing to support the scientific facts." He loves the wolf and he loves nature, but sadness is in Julio's voice as he ponders whether our efforts are too late. Should he have pushed harder, earlier? He says, "Let's have a big honest effort to save the wild animal. If you want to save the wolf, you must save the land." His love for the wilds and for the wolf are genuine and emotional. "I would prefer to see the last Mexican wolf die in a trap or by poison, rather than see the last ten to twelve in a cage."

I would prefer to see the last Mexican wolf die in a trap or by poison, rather than see the last ten to twelve in a cage

Since our conversation, Julio has remained committed to the wolf, but he has changed jobs and has dedicated his work to the development of environmental education. As the director of Proteccion de la Fauna Mexicana A.C., he trains survey biologists for Mexican field studies. He also works to train teachers, and beyond that to influence the future. Julio understands that effective regulation is based on people's acceptance of limits and their desire to protect the environment because it is important to them.

8

Middle Eastern Wolves

THE WOLF IS A holarctic northern species. From Minnesota to Maine, it is referred to as the Eastern timber wolf. It's a subspecies of the gray wolf, which ranges throughout North America, Europe, and Asia. Throughout the northern hemisphere, all wolves, with the possible exception of the red wolf, are varieties of a single species.

Subspecies are identified by a geographic area, so that in North America we have the Mexican wolf, the Rocky Mountain wolf, the prairie wolf, the Eastern timber wolf, the arctic wolf, and the MacKenzie Valley wolf. Worldwide, wolves range in size from the forty-pound (18.2 kg) variety in Israel and Saudi Arabia to the MacKenzie Valley wolves, which easily reach over one hundred pounds (45 kg). Populations of wolves in other parts of the world are subject to the same pressures that have eliminated the wolves in most of the United States.

Small wolves exist in all countries of the Middle East. They feed primarily on domestic animals and garbage, and are legally protected only in Israel. There are four subspecies within the area. The world's smallest wolf is in most of the Arabian Peninsula, south Sinai, southern Israel, and southern Jordan.

Iyad Nader, a researcher in Saudi Arabia, told us that originally the wolves were thought to be very rare. He guesses that there may be a few hundred in the Middle East. They had thought that wolves would be most abundant in the west and southwest, where the biological diversity is greater, but reports showed the wolves in the desert of the central parts were at least equal in population density. Some of the larger populations exist in mountainous regions.

The wolves in this area are widely dispersed, usually living alone or in pairs. In comparison with statistical information that we have in North America, there are very few, if any, official records of wolves being shot. This does not mean that shooting is not a factor, however. It is commonplace for desert dwellers to have guns with them at all times and there is no place for the wolf to hide. There are no restrictions on shooting in Saudi Arabia, even though the Natural Resources Commission has the wolf on its list of protected animals. Another factor is that there is a problem with feral dogs in the region, and the wolf is sure to suffer from the poison used for the dogs.

Heinrich Mendelssohn of Tel-Aviv University confirms that the Middle East's four different wolf subspecies all have populations in Israel, where they are protected by law. The different varieties decrease in size from north to south, becoming darker and larger where there is more rainfall. The southern subspecies survives without drinking water. All successful animals in a desert surrounding must find an adaptation to deal with the lack of water. The wolf derives most of its fluids from its prey, but in the area near Eilat the wolves have taken to consuming overripe watermelon in the local dump. While this cannot be described as a common strategy, it does suggest that the wolves are willing to use any expedient means to address their liquid needs. Most Israeli wolves are scavengers living at garbage dumps. Because they scavenge road kills as well, they are in jeopardy while feeding; the major cause of mortality for Israeli wolves is car collisions.

Israeli wolves are pressured by increased human settlement, and even though the Hebrew tradition does not include the same degree of animosity toward the wolf that is common in Europe and North America, there is still a conflict. Heinrich Mendelssohn states in his essay "Wolves in Israel," "If, however, wolves preyed upon livestock, the farmers poisoned the wolves, advised by pest control officers who encouraged wholesale application of poisons." Unfortunately, this is an all-too-common solution. The government is attempting to eliminate this thirty-year-old procedure by paying farmers for livestock loss. Without this kind of support, wolves in Israel have a very uncertain future.

Iyad Nader

Iyad Nader came to Saudi Arabia in 1971 from Baghdad, Iraq. He is Director of Natural Resources in Saudi Arabia and a member of the national commission that is trying to conserve the remaining components of Saudi Arabia's flora and fauna, so his concern must be for all animals.

Nader's wolf research is mostly anecdotal. "I have always been interested in animals," he tells us. "When I was young, we lived in the city, but we had a garden and I had a few pet animals in the backyard. Later when I graduated from high school, I really wanted to be a doctor. I was not successful, so I got into the College of Education, Department of Biology. I was a teacher in Baghdad. My father was a teacher, my mother was a teacher—we were a family of teachers. My older brother is a teacher at the University of Baghdad. Later, after graduating from college, I got a government scholarship to get my master's and Ph.D. in the States. I went to the Department of Zoology in Illinois. I got my Ph.D. on the taxonomy of two species of kangaroo rats of the southwest, in Mexico. We had field trips down south. This is why I chose the topic—more reminiscent of my home country."

He tells of places in southwest Saudi Arabia where people still shoot wolves and hang them from the branches of a tree or on a post. Since many of these incidents are simply word-of-mouth accounts, few are included in the official wolf statistics. As the work in Montana has demonstrated, however, we should not disregard these reports. The legs of shot wolves are tied and a little piece of paper is left next to them, or nailed to them, proudly identifying the person who killed the wolf. Although it is not clear exactly why, wolves' connection with evil in so many legends suggests that the power of a wolf's gaze may have something to do with the evil eye. Hence, displaying the dead wolf in this manner may serve some other purpose than just boosting the hunter's ego.

In the Middle East the wolf has suffered from the additional pressure of numerous wars, deforestation, indiscriminate shooting, and starvation. The signing of peace accords in the Middle East may allow the wolf and other wildlife to prosper again throughout the region. Studies have been hampered by wars, border conflicts, land mines, suspicions. We know that there were large numbers of animals killed for food and by accident during the various conflicts, but there are no records of what and how many. We do not know of incidental death from the land mines and bombings. We know that the poisons used in the Golan Heights to control wolf-dog hybrids have eliminated the wolf in the area, but we don't know how many areas have used this technique. Peace is something we have all prayed for. Now that we have it, we can only assume that the animals would like to celebrate too.

9

Wolves of Southern Europe

WOLVES ARE FOUND on the Iberian Peninsula in Spain and Portugal, in Italy, and in Greece. The last wolf to be seen in France before 1993 was an eighty-four-pound (38-kg) male killed by a man hunting wild boar in the French Alps on December 27, 1987. The hunter did not know at the time that he had killed a wolf. The only other reports of wolves in France, since World War Two, are from 1977 and 1993.

In 1840, wolves lived all over Spain, but by 1940, they occupied only one-half of their former range. Now the wolves live in the northwestern quarter of the country on dry, high plateaus from the Atlantic to the Sierra de Cameros and in two isolated areas in the Sierra de Gata and the San Pedros. Where the wolves live, the temperature ranges from 14 to 86 degrees Fahrenheit (- 10° to 30° C). Newspaper accounts in 1991 put Spain's wolf population between 1,470 and 2,058 animals, but estimates are exaggerated every time there is a domestic livestock loss. In recent years, wolves in the northern part of the range have seen a population increase, while the southern populations have fallen.

In 1989, the Iberian wolf was given full protection in Portugal. In the first two months of 1990, thirteen were killed illegally, and one was run over. The entire population of wolves in Portugal is somewhere under two hundred. They are found mainly in the northern region of Portugal along the border with Spain, with a sparse population in the southern part of the country.

Italy has perhaps the most well-studied wolves in Europe. The population of 300 to 350 animals is less than that of the Iberian Peninsula, but exceeds that of the Scandinavian countries and is comparable to the population in Greece. The wolves live in the hill country of central Italy, where — as in all of southern Europe — interactions with free-ranging and feral dogs make hybridization a potential threat to the survival of the species.

Luigi Boitani

Luigi Boitani's work in central Italy began in 1973 and now includes radio telemetry. He explains how his study began. "Everything happened just by chance. I had returned to Italy from a period of studying in North America, and I was looking around for a new topic to research. I just got my position at the university, and during this search I came across the WWF [World Wildlife Fund] concern with the wolf. They knew that the wolf was possibly an endangered species and, most importantly, there was very little information on the wolves' status [in Italy]. So that's what happened. They asked me if I was interested in that and I said, 'Yes, sure.'

"The WWF was the major contributor for the first ten years of my project, and I think it's been one of the longest lasting projects that WWF has ever funded all over the world. [Finally] WWF gave up, and actually I was one of the supporters of WWF giving up, for after all WWF is not a research center. They have to be a catalyst for new research and they have to put seed money, but they don't have to support long-term projects. So, anyway, they gave up and I found other funds through the university, private donors, the National Institute of Wildlife Biology in Italy, other international support, and regional governments. The wolf is a spectacular species, very charismatic. It's very easy to sell the image, and also it's a controversial species. The wolf unfortunately makes a lot of damage to livestock, so this forces government into paying something to try and find the solution. At the moment, for example, I've never been so rich in research funds."

Boitani continues, "When we began we found the situation was rather desperate. Nothing was known. No single paper ever written on Italian wolves, and the question we had from WWF was, How many and where? How do you look for wolves in a country like Italy? So we start a search for indirect information by talking with people, visiting areas, all sorts of indirect means. Then we had a field census. There were a lot of people in a few days on the snow searching for wolf tracks, and we had a ratio calculated to evaluate all our indirect information. So we came up with a figure and a distribution area.

"That was the real beginning. Then we thought immediately that we had to go on for a more intensive search . . . , and we went on radio tracking. But radio tracking in Italy is something different from radio tracking in the U.S. We always use radios as a means to get to the animal, to follow it on the snow, to observe indirectly. In twenty years we have used planes or helicopters perhaps ten times. We walk, we ski, and we drive. There are roads going many places, and then you walk to vantage points and you can watch the animals. It's a mountain area, and flying would be of very little use."

There are an estimated 200,000 strays, 80,000 feral, and 800,000 free-ranging pet dogs in Italy. They compete for food and interbreed with wolves, which weakens the wolves' genetic purity. Luigi has radio collared known hybrids that have had all the outward behaviors of wolves. Animal protection groups vehemently object to any form of control over these dog populations, and it is possible that captive breeding might be needed to keep a pure wolf lineage—if one still exists.

Luigi explains the dog situation. "It's a major threat. That's certainly true. Italy's full of free-ranging dogs. These free-ranging animals are coming from at least three different sources. The first ones are stray dogs, animals that had an owner at some time in their lives, and they hang around the edges of humans' houses looking for a new master.

"Then there are the feral ones—animals that have abandoned any relationship with humans. They live outside in the forest and they live like wolves. They have the same ecology. We have been trapping, collaring, and studying them and we have found out some interesting results. From an ecological point of view they are very, very similar to wolves. They eat the same. They move in the same pattern. They have a tremendous advantage when you think that all females reproduce, while in a wolf pack, only one female usually will reproduce. They have two breeding seasons in a year, not only one.

So there is tremendous potential for increase. Fortunately, the odds of mortality are very high, because they are not really well fit to a natural environment, so the first winter takes a heavy toll.

"The third source of free-ranging animals are those that have an owner somewhere, but the owner just doesn't care and leaves them free to roam where they want, which is the normal way of keeping dogs in many villages in mountain areas. Sometimes for climatic reasons, sometimes for cultural reasons, dogs are considered something that is part of the community, even if there is a master somewhere that takes care of them, but they are left free in the village. This means that if a female in heat passes by, all the dogs go up into the forest for a day, maybe several kilometers, so ecologically they are a potential threat to all wildlife. We have evidence of interbreeding wolves with these dogs. Of course this would be a major problem. Then the wolf gene pool would be wiped out, or at least swamped, by the dogs."

The wolf population in Italy was only one hundred in 1973, but a ban on poisons in 1976 may have been responsible for the current increase. As a result, the wolf has expanded its range and Luigi's research area has expanded as well. One rumor that persists, however, despite its obvious error, is that wolves are being introduced from Canada and Siberia.

Italian wolves rely on the beech forests and higher elevations for protection. Like animals all over the world, habitat and natural prey are the key ingredients to survival, but like the Israeli wolves, these wolves have turned to garbage for the majority of their food.

Luigi describes the wolves' feeding and other behavioral habits. "Their major prey is small game or garbage that they found at the open dumps, and so there is no need to go in the pack and to hunt for garbage. They prefer to go alone. They have quite a bit of interaction with other wildlife or domestic animals going to the dumps, not with humans. In Italy wolves know very well what humans are and what they do, how they behave, how dangerous they are. In Italy wolves learn how to avoid all those dangers. That's a big advantage. They have been persecuted for centuries, so in certain ways they've been selected to be extremely cautious.

"There are park areas and natural areas, but they certainly are too small to contain any viable population of wolves. So the wolves survive in Italy because they are anywhere, regardless of the protection status of a certain area. Concerning the fact that the wolf is a wilderness beast, I would oppose that totally. Not only because in Italy we have the best evidence that the wolves can live anywhere, even close to human villages. I also oppose that on philosophical grounds. We have to think of the wolf as a potential companion in any kind of habitat, not only in wilderness."

We ask Luigi how wolves managed to survive in Italy when they were wiped out of other European countries. He replies, "Well, this is a very long story. I have a theory or a hypothesis that cannot be proved, but most probably what made the difference is the different attitudes that Italians have toward the wolves. Not only Italians, but in general the Mediterranean people. They have an ambiguous/positive attitude, contrasting the negative attitudes of the central European people. This probably led to a less intensive and organized hunt on Italian wolves.

"Also the geographical and ecological heterogeneity of Italy would have made a difference. There were high mountains where agriculture is not really possible. So wolves would have huge areas where they can live alone, but this was in the past, of course. Then all the wild prey had been wiped out, so the wolves had no reason to stay in these huge wooded areas and they had to come down and close to the villages and that's how they learned to live nearby humans.

> *We have to think of the wolf as a potential companion in any kind of habitat, not only in wilderness*

"In Italy, the attitudes toward the wolf in the classical time were quite positive. At least they were not very negative, which is already quite a good achievement," he says with a chuckle. "Many classical authors are referring to the wolf in . . . positive terms. They were considering the animal as just a component of the natural environment, sometimes making some damage, but like lightning will do, so not any really negative reaction.

"Even before the Romans, the Italian people have been selecting for a guard dog which you will probably start to learn about in the U.S. and in Canada. These dogs have been brought here for starting a new anti-predator program. They are a mastiff-type guard dog, selected to defend herds from the wolf, but they are not selected to hunt and kill the wolf, which is a very important cultural difference. We accept the wolf out there as long as it doesn't harm too much, and this probably made the difference for the wolves' survival."

Luigi is quite animated as he lets his theory unfold. "Unfortunately, the dominant culture after Roman and Classical time was the Church, and the Church brought in a very negative attitude. Let's not forget that the Church had its cultural basis in the Bible and the Bible was written by nomadic shepherds in the Middle East. They had a very negative attitude toward the wolf, and the Church was then responsible for bringing this negative attitude and spreading it with all the power of the Church."

When we ask Luigi if he has learned anything unexpected, he says, "Well, for example, the pattern of movement. The wolves in Italy are totally nocturnal. During the day they sleep and rest. [They] don't move at all. This is an obvious adaptation to human presence. Then they have rendezvous sites or resting sites, retreat areas we call them, usually in the forest area, where there is vegetation cover and they can hide. Then at sunset they move and come down to the bottom of the valleys looking for food. This could be garbage at the dump, could be livestock—sheep yard—could be small game. Basically this is the pattern. Then at sunrise, the wolves go back up into their retreat areas, which are not far, maybe one or two kilometers away from the village. There are villages everywhere in Italy. You shouldn't forget that Italy has a mean human density of 185 persons per square kilometer [481 persons per square mile]."

We ask about the major threats to wolves and their existence in Italy. Luigi responds, "At the moment the major threat is that wolves are killed by hunters, just by accident. But I have to explain that. There are no hunters going for the wolves, but there are many hunters around, hunting some other kind of game and when they see a wolf they will shoot without thinking twice that the animal is indeed fully protected, since '76. This is a major cause of mortality. Then there are still some illegal uses of poison baits—cyanides and strychnine. Then you wouldn't believe it but car accidents have taken quite a toll, especially on young animals, one year olds, when they start to leave mama and father and wander alone, and they don't know much about roads and cars."

To protect the wolves' future, there is now a compensation program for farmers in some districts and a program to reestablish the wolves' natural prey species. This program is complicated by the fact that 50 percent of the losses are due to domestic dogs. Luigi is also working for practical changes in sheep farming. He would like to make the compensation available only to people who use sheep dogs.

The good news is that people in Italy have been abandoning the mountains, and the forests are coming back. Pastures are being restored and wildlife is returning. In a country where conservation and environmental education are unknown, population and development are tremendous, and preservation of natural areas is almost non-existent, we must grab any opportunity to promote an environmental ethic.

Javier Castroviejo

Javier Castroviejo is a Spanish researcher. He laughs about Scandinavian wolf discussions and all of their science and theories. "They have all the intelligence, but we have all the wolves," he says. The wolf battles folklore in Spain, as it does in most of its European range. According to Javier, "Our countrymen say that when a wolf is following you, you know, because your hair is up and you get chicken skin [goose bumps]. Sometimes really, it makes an impression in the lonely mountains to hear a wolf howling. You are alone and it makes you feel very small. Even from a car, you hear the family howling in the night and it's something to remember. In times when there was no electric power, you saw strange things—people with abnormalities like too much hair. You can think very easily that they were werewolves. Our people say that a wolf can go for weeks without eating anything, only grass, clay, or mud."

A 1991 newspaper article cited changes in attitude as one of the primary factors in wolf survival. They were protected by law in 1971 and a prohibition on poison bait was introduced in 1980. There was also a resurgence in natural prey, which reduced livestock depredation. Still, a hundred wolves a year might be shot, trapped, run over, or poisoned illegally. According to a 1990 Spanish newspaper account, 20 percent of the animals killed were pups caught in the wild.

Restrictions on hunting practices and depredation payments are necessary for wolf survival in Spain, although some problems are aggravated by unhealthy livestock or poorly disposed of carcasses. Wolves also suffer from innuendo. The following is a quote from a Spanish newspaper. "The wolves found the cattle about 7:30 Saturday morning and even though the wolves were not actually confirmed, the neighbors assured that the wolves had been on the slopes of the mountains." Overall, the wolves, like so many of the European examples, rely on garbage and carrion to survive.

Javier has brought some order into the study of wolves in Spain. His father and grandfather were professors of law who liked to hunt partridge and woodcock with their dogs. Javier became intrigued with all animals through the books in the family library. His father was an author and infused a love of books in the young boy. In addition, his father considered the wolf to be a persecuted, but mythic, animal and he was very fond of it.

Javier's first research was on a game bird, but the howling of the wolves near the research area changed his life. While he was researching the capercaillie in the Spanish mountains, people wondered why he expended so much energy studying a bird. He arose at 1:00 or 2:00 in the morning to run to the mountains, looking for the bird's display, and returned by 11:00 A.M. Rumors had him going to meet his many girlfriends in the village, then shifted to rumors of contraband, and finally to a religious offering.

Research takes many twists, and Javier remembers one very dramatic event. "I had friends [who were] killed in Bolivia, because of the drug traffic. We were making an exploration in a very remote area of northeast Bolivia, on the border with Brazil. It was a high mountain area where there was not supposed to be people—a safe, brief geological expedition. Before they went to establish a camp there, a pilot, a Bolivian professional, and my friend found this small airfield. They landed there and saw a small camp. Two went there and two waited in the airplane. The two that went [to the camp] came [back] with two other people with machine guns. They were the guardians of the cocaine industry. The survivor told me he tried to explain that they were not police, but the drug people thought the guide had a pistol. They began to shoot, and the pilot and my friend ran through the airfield into the jungle and stopped—motionless, despite mosquitoes and everything, from 1:00 midday until 5:00 the next day, not making a single movement, even to see the airplane. He saw the two people with the machine guns looking for him. The next day, when [it was] still dark, he saw the pilot killed in the airfield. The plane was burned. We don't know how he decided to step into the airfield. He thought other planes would come and see the plane, and think it was an accident and land. Another plane landed and he escaped with them."

Luckily, Javier has not had to contend with this kind of adventure at home, where he enjoys the campfire stories told of wolves and is moved by the sound of wolf howls. He has heard stories about the wolf's bite, which, according to local belief, has a poison in it that paralyzes its victims. He has heard about the shepherd who saw one of his sheep being attacked by a wolf. The shepherd ran out to the sheep, and man and wolf engaged in a tug-o-war with a lamb. When the man won, the wolf lurched forward, getting the shepherd's nose in its mouth. The startled animal left an impression on the man's skin but did not bite. The wolf ran off.

Javier has attempted to put knowledge in place of folklore and story. The following, from a 1991 Spanish newspaper article, suggests he has a challenge before him.

A group of wolves has killed a herd of sheep on the snowy mountains in the north of Spain. The owners, people who are not rich, complained because the laws do not permit them to kill the carnivores in defense of their helpless herds. Without a doubt, few wolves remain and they need protection to maintain ecological balance, but will they be able to maintain the wolves from becoming endangered species if the sheep are at the mercy of their voracity and the owners must stand by and generously accept their losses?

Jan van Haaften

Jan van Haaften is from the Netherlands, a country with no wolf population, but this has not stopped him from becoming a wolf scientist.

In 1975, Jan began research in Portugal. The International Union of Game Biologists met in Lisbon, and this allowed Jan to see the potential and need for his work. His questions were, How can the Iberian wolf be sufficiently protected? What can be done to prevent wolf damage to domestic animals? What measures can be taken to protect roe deer and other potential prey populations?

Jan was born in 1927 in the village of Ziest, where he grew up with stories of *Little Red Riding Hood* and *The Wolf and the Seven Goats.* The wolf was always the bad guy. Jan's father was an engineer who worked on the country's dike system. Traveling with him broadened Jan's horizons but did not tell him what he wanted to do for a career. However, Jan unknowingly learned many of his research techniques on his father's hunting land, where he mapped all the locations of game.

When Jan was in his early teens the Nazis controlled his country. He worked in a photography shop and literally hid in the darkroom during the days. His father had been on the town board and had to hide from the Germans. His mother was a pianist and infused music into his life. Biology was his hobby, but his main interest was music and he attended the Conservatory to study it.

His father was not supportive of this plan, however, so Jan decided to switch to theology. He quickly found that the priesthood was not his calling, so he began his third degree program, this time in biology, and appealed to his father again. "I asked him if it was possible for me to go to the Conservatorium to study music, singing especially, and the violin. He said, 'Only when you also finish your biology study.' So I did both. It took me two years longer than normal, but anyhow I did, and I had great fun. I still do have. I think it's good that you are not only biologists, but that you have something else besides."

Jan's life has been filled with changes of direction. Because he is open to new ideas and has such a broad interest base, his life can be hard to follow, but it is never dull. Even the choice of a wife was unconventional by most standards. "I was on the Board of the Netherlands Christian Student Society and I had to make a big party for the first-year students," he remembers. "I told them to make pancakes, and I asked the girls of the first-year students to come. I'm always, when I make an appointment, exactly on time, but nobody was there. I went out and had a look, and then my wife came. Well I didn't know her, but I saw a girl coming with a pan in her hand to make pancakes. I saw her and I thought, 'Well, that's my wife.'"

Jan laughs and continues, "Actually, it took quite a long time. We got more and more in touch with each other, but well, we were young, so we had the time, and I was very old-fashioned. I didn't want to marry before I was ready with my study. She studied first sociology, then she went on a course for a secretary, which was very good for me because she could typewrite very good."

Jan's biology degree included a specialty in endocrinology. He worked at the hospital for nine months, but found himself getting too involved with his patients to be a doctor. When he got married, his wife pointed out that he was only home when he was worn out, so he shifted careers. The next twist was work at the Physiological Institute, where he studied a compound in grasses and clover that has properties similar to estrogen. The result was his first doctorate. His supervisor was what he calls, a "school teacher." Despite Jan's late hours, his boss would stand at the door, point to his watch, and say, "You're five minutes late."

He eventually got a position in the Department of Game Research in 1958, and within ten years he was department head. He worked on roe deer, seals, pheasants, hares, and fox during his years there. In 1968, he became the first European to use radio telemetry to track animals. In 1973, he was employed by the university and still maintained his position at the Game Institute. At the university, a Portuguese student piqued his interest in the Iberian wolf, and by the 1975 IUCN conference, Jan was ready to make a proposal.

David Mech reviewed the proposal and encouraged Jan. In addition, Dave agreed to advise the project. It soon became obvious that there was no field researcher available in Portugal at that time, so Jan arranged for a sabbatical in 1982, and the research commenced. Among his assistants was Francisco Fonseca. The work took place in the mountains of Portugal, eighty-five miles (136 km) from the Atlantic Ocean.

The mountain summits in the research area are bare and rocky, and the slopes are covered with oak and pine. Sheep dogs, hunting dogs, and strays all roam the area. Perhaps the most difficult wolf management problem at that time was the status of dogs. The Portuguese are allowed to use up to ten dogs for hunting, and packs of stray (feral) dogs are a threat to wolves, livestock, and prey. However, all dogs have a special respect and protection, and it is illegal to kill them.

Part of Jan's research was based on a survey of local citizens. This survey provided insight into attitudes and beliefs, as well as into wolf distribution. The accounts he gathered do not give a picture of the wolf as a man-eater. Numerous stories were told about wolves attacking men riding donkeys, then backing off when they realized there was a rider. In other stories of attacks on people, the wolf was always driven off by noise or sticks. The attacks appear to be accidental meetings, and the wolves always gave up. It is also possible that these attacks might have been made by stray dogs and not by wolves at all. Only two incidents describe wolves killing and eating a human. One involved an alcoholic woman found outside her village and the second a shepherd who disappeared from his flock. Both stories are based on supposition rather than on fact, however, and both could be more dog-related events.

Jan undertook his second doctorate in Yugoslavia in 1964 on roe deer. After his wolf research in Portugal, he returned to Yugoslavia, where he fought the politics of the Eastern Bloc in order to study wolves there. Jan explains, "They said, 'Well, we really don't know anything about them. We only know that they are here and some people don't like them.' Then I started to get in touch with several people to learn more about wolves in Yugoslavia. A friend of mine in Zagreb was studying the brown bear. We started to work together studying the wolf and the brown bear in the same area. I would give some lectures and then I could go into the national park and study with my students. We were kicked out by the police after two years.

"My students were used to being free to do everything they like and they were told by the police that they were not allowed to go here, or to go there, and so on. One time they went into the woods checking the wolves and they came in an area where they were not allowed. You couldn't see it when you were entering that area in the woods itself, only when you were coming by car. They went in the wrong area, just working, and the police took them. They said, 'Well you must leave the country in twenty-four hours.' They called me by telephone and asked, 'What shall we do?' I told them, 'Please go, because otherwise it is going to be difficult to get you out of jail in these countries.' They went out of Yugoslavia and they got the message [that] they were not allowed to come into Yugoslavia again for two years. I went back the next year and tried to set up a new project with all the students there, but they didn't allow me. They even kicked my friend out of Zagreb. He found a new area, a bit easier to reach, but there are no wolves around."

As for the Netherlands, Jan doesn't believe there is any future for wolves there. "In our country, the woodland part is only 7 percent of the whole country. It is in the center, but full of roads, full of fences. There are people living all around with their domestic livestock. The wolf will not do what everybody thinks they have to do. They will not eat just roe deer. They are going to take cows. They would get a lot of problems with our traffic, which is very heavy. When you have a very small group of wolves, you get inbreeding. We see that already in zoos. In our country there is a zoo where we saw that after several years the cubs were not healthy any longer. There are no wolves in Germany, there are no wolves in Belgium, so if they're not in our neighboring countries, they don't have the chance to contact other populations. I told them in Holland, and I told television, that I am against reintroduction because of that."

In 1992 a single wolf was sighted in the former East German countryside. This was an exciting event and has inspired German wolf interest, but it's not enough to change Jan's premise.

Francisco Fonseca

Portuguese wolves face the same problems as all the other wolves of Europe: habitat destruction, loss of natural prey species, poaching, and a lack of understanding of the species by the general public. In the wolf's favor is Grupo Lobo, which was founded in 1985 to work for the conservation of the species. Francisco (Chico) Fonseca, a wolf researcher and professor at Lisbon University, was the driving force behind the formation of the non-profit, non-governmental organization.

During his years of research in the field, it became apparent to Francisco that there was a great need for an educational campaign to inform the people of Portugal about the true nature of the wolf. Like many non-profit educational organizations, Grupo Lobo has struggled to maintain its existence, but it has so far been funded to do research into causes of sheep mortality, which would help the shepherds and their flocks, as well as the wolves. "The public doesn't know anything about the wolf—why they kill so many sheep, for example. It's because they have no natural prey. We can avoid so much damage, but people don't care about that. It's easier to kill the wolves than to look for solutions to the problem," Francisco says with frustration.

Grupo Lobo has submitted a proposal to the European Economic Community for measures to avoid such damage, and they are waiting for approval for the project from the Portuguese National Park Service. Other grants have allowed them to develop an educational exhibit that was on display in Lisbon for the benefit of school children and the general public. Grupo Lobo also tries to rescue wolves that are captured and kept illegally by people. Many times the animals are injured and in need of special care.

According to Fonseca, the situation of the Iberian wolf is similar to the situation that exists in North America, where wolves migrate back and forth across the Canadian/U.S. border. Iberian wolves in Portugal are mainly found in the northern region along the border with Spain, with a sparse population in the southern part of the country.

It's easier to kill the wolves than to look for solutions to the problem

Francisco Fonseca was born in the city, but spent much of his childhood weekends and holidays on a farm. His parents enjoyed the countryside and loved animals. This love was passed on to Chico, but his strongest interest was in the big predators. "When I was younger, I heard everyone speak about wolves," he recalls. "I remember one day, when I was about five or six years old, we were coming back from a wedding near the top of our highest mountain. I heard someone in the car say, 'Oh, look. A wolf.' It was passing in front of our car. I saw something very similar to a dog, but I don't know if it was a wolf or not. I was too young."

OPPOSITE: *The red wolf* (Canis rufus) *is the wolf of the southeastern United States. Declared biologically extinct in the wild in 1980, the red wolf is now making a comeback through captive breeding programs.*

OPPOSITE INSET: *North Carolina's Alligator River National Wildlife Refuge reintroduction camp for red wolves. This project is important to all species that might need to be reintroduced to the wilds from zoo stock.*

ABOVE LEFT: *Weighing wolves for transplant to Michigan. This experiment was a failure, but we have learned from it and other studies. Potential success for a relocation is much greater today.*

ABOVE RIGHT: *For reintroduction programs it sometimes is necessary to recapture animals that stray from the chosen site. The capture collar allows scientists to track animals and to inject them with a tranquilizer by radio signal.*

ABOVE: *Wild wolves eating caribou in Alaska's Denali National Park and Preserve. The wolves' diet is varied, but they rely on the large ungulates for their primary sustenance.*

RIGHT: *A freshly car-killed deer provides supper for this captive wolf. The wolf was part of a recent study at Northern Michigan University.*

FAR RIGHT: *Rolf Peterson examining wolf remains. There are many clues to perplexing questions within the skeletal remains of the wolf. Wolf researchers ask the questions and decipher the answers.*

FAR LEFT: *When a wolf is trapped, one of the first things that scientists check for is sticks in the wolf's mouth. The animal may bite at branches in frustration and confusion and the results could be serious if the researcher fails to notice.*

LEFT: *Researcher Fred Harrington crouches to stock a food cache. Later, the captive wolf shown ate the food and scent-marked the cache. The experiment helped the researchers to conclude that wolves practiced scent-marking at a food site, similar to the behavior of foxes and coyotes.*

ABOVE: *The wolf howl has many different purposes; only another wolf can fully interpret the meanings.*

TOP: *Wolf shot in Michigan's Upper Peninsula. It was an unfortunate ending for one of the unsuccessful animals in the first translocation experiment.*

LEFT: *The shooting of wolves is illegal in the lower forty-eight United States. A federal predator control specialist is required to remove problem wolves.*

ABOVE RIGHT: *Minnesota's Kawishiwi Lodge, home to the Superior National Forest researchers since 1966.*

Chico is passionate about wolves and his enthusiasm is evident as he recalls, "When I was young I heard everybody blame the wolf for everything, saying it is not good for anything. Then in 1977 when I started an investigation of the local people to know what they think about wolves, I am very surprised when I ask a shepherd if wolves are necessary. He said, 'Yes, they are necessary.' It is a big surprise to me, because until now, I only have the answer, 'No, the wolf is not necessary. We must destroy him.' I asked [the shepherd] why the wolf is necessary and he said, 'It is necessary to defend the property. If the wolf didn't exist, the shepherds would not care about the sheep and they would go everywhere and destroy everything. So we must have wolves to oblige the shepherds to be careful and take care of the sheep."

Chico began his research in 1977 after finishing a degree in biology. A year in the field or lab was required, and a professor suggested that he work on wolves. Since that was his long-held dream, he accepted the challenge. One of the initial goals of his study was to determine the distribution of the wolves in Portugal. A survey was done of the people who lived in the countryside or worked in the forests. They were asked if they had seen wolves, or dens, how many males, and how many females.

At first, people responded aggressively when Chico spoke to them about wolves. "Everything depends on the way you speak with them," he says. "I found especially the older people are more against the wolves, but when you speak with them calmly, after a few minutes they are very friendly."

When Chico and his assistants go into the field, they stay there for twenty to twenty-five days. They collect scats and try to locate tracks and dead animals. "There is a dead wolf in the surroundings most of the time. We collect wolf carcasses and sometimes only a skull or bone. The wolf is a magnificent animal, a beautiful animal. The first time I saw a dead wolf, it was awful to me. Even now, I don't like to see them dead," Chico tells us, and his voice echoes with obvious hurt.

The researchers have tried radio tracking on a small scale, but trapping wolves is very difficult. In the study conducted by Jan van Haaften, it was found that wolves were very suspicious around snares baited with carrion. Any changes in the immediate surroundings, such as cutting of trees or shrubs, made them wary. Human scent may have also warned the wolves. At one point the researchers boiled the snares in a pan filled with water and forest fruits to give them a natural scent, and they wore gloves when handling the snares, but even these precautions yielded little success. Most often they caught fox and feral and domestic dogs.

Fonseca tells us that tracking is difficult in Portugal. "One of our biggest problems is that there are very few days of snow. Maybe a week where we have real snow, where we can track animals, and then it's completely different. In one day we saw so many tracks of wolves, fox, badger, and so on, it was unbelievable! It's very hard to work with sand prints. Very bad." After they have collected their data and samples in the field, they return to the lab in Lisbon to analyze the information. "You don't realize how much you've collected until you get back to the lab and get everything organized," he says.

Francisco realizes the necessity and importance of lab work, but his heart is in the field,. "You become a new man when you go to the field. To return to the city, it's awful. I'm in my office every day, writing and writing. Sometimes you are looking at the TV and you see the places that you work and you wish to be there."

Francisco recalls his first encounters with wolves. "The first time I heard howling, I was in bed. I had a little window open and I hear something from outside. I don't know [what it is]. 'It's a wolf. No, it's impossible. Yes, it's a wolf.' It's in the winter and too cold, so I close the window." He could still hear the howling, but hardly believed his ears. Then he heard a wolf howl and another answer back and he believed.

On another occasion he heard a dog barking and the ringing of bells worn by sheep. He was outside and turned to see a dark brown animal far away. It could have been a fox. It was running toward him and kept getting closer until finally he could see it was a wolf. He still heard the dog barking, and suddenly he saw that the dog was chasing the wolf. Just as suddenly, the wolf leapt to its right and disappeared into some bushes. Francisco could see it come to an open field, and it seemed to pause and wait for the dog. When the dog came to where the wolf had jumped into the brush, it stopped, but continued barking. Francisco could see the wolf waiting, and to his eyes it appeared as if the wolf was thinking, 'Come here, boy.' Then the wolf crossed the field and as Chico says, "The dog decided it's crazy to be here barking and barking, so he went away also."

Many times when the researchers are looking at tracks, they are not certain whether they belong to wolves or to feral dogs. The latter are a very big problem in Portugal. There are thousands of them roaming the countryside. After hunting season, if hunters can't retrieve their dogs, they leave them to fend for themselves. The dogs begin to hunt the same food that the wolves depend on. Feral dogs will attack sheep, cows, goats, and red deer, and many times wolves are blamed for these attacks.

Farmers are compensated for losses due to wolf depredation, but according to Francisco, "Since the local authorities started to pay for the damage done by wolves, there are no livestock that have died from natural causes. All of them are from attacks of wolves! And we have also found that people have lied about animals that have died. We have been advised by the local veterinarian for example, that a cow was dead in a certain place. In a few days a man appears and says, 'Oh, my cow was killed by a wolf.' The man in charge of the investigation asks, 'You are sure that it was a wolf?' 'Yes, I'm sure.' 'This is not true, because we have already been advised by the veterinarian that your cow died from disease.'"

The wolves' most common natural prey in Portugal are rabbit and roe deer. The red deer was also a traditional prey species, but it has been absent from Portugal for some years until a recent influx from Spain. Wolves will also eat wild boar. In one instance, Francisco talked to a shepherd who saw four wolves attacking a wild boar. The shepherd and some associates made a lot of noise and scared the wolves away and then took the boar for themselves.

The authorities in a position to make decisions about habitat protection and prey species know that in order to protect and preserve the Iberian wolf, an effort must be made to improve the natural prey situation and to set aside large enough amounts of land to act as preserves for the wolf. As yet the authorities have not taken the necessary steps to insure this. It is often a frustrating and difficult struggle to work for the preservation of a species, but Francisco Fonseca is willing to pursue the cause. He says, "My father says I always liked lost causes. But I don't think it's true."

10

Wolves of Poland

RESEARCH ON POLISH wolves has until recently been limited to the study of their predation on red deer. In 1991, researcher Katarzyna Kubzdela hoped to begin a comprehensive long-term study of the biology and behavior of the Polish wolf, leading to a complete conservation plan. The funding did not come through for a variety of reasons and the project had to be abandoned, but her request pointed out the limitations of and possible errors in the existing data and the need for specialized study.

Bugoslav Bobek

Until further research is undertaken in Poland, we have the limited information gathered by Bugoslav Bobek, head of the department of wildlife research at the University of Krakow. Bobek began his research in the early seventies while working with red deer in the Carpathian Mountains. In the process of the study he became interested in learning more about the impact of wolves on red deer mortality. At the time, biologists believed that the wolves were killing only the poorer quality deer, while hunters and foresters believed wolves were more random in their kills, taking healthy as well as sickly animals.

Bobek used the analysis of bone marrow fat on the deer remains to determine their health, and though he admits that this is not always the best index to use, it was the only one available at the time. The results of this study stated an "interesting pattern of wolf predation. You have two peaks. One is animals in really poor condition [where] fat content in the tibia [leg bone] was 10 to 20 percent, no more. Then there was a gap and a second peak where animals had 80 to 90 percent of fat in the tibia. Very healthy."

Bobek speculates that there are two possible explanations. One is that when wolves chase a group of deer, they separate out the slower, weaker ones who do not have enough energy to keep up with the group. As for the animals with good fat reserves, Bugoslav speculates that this may be their downfall also, because they cannot exchange heat efficiently and they become tired easily.

By following tracks in the snow, researchers learned that the wolves were forcing the deer to run down steep valleys. Working as a team, one group of wolves runs along the edge of the valley and the other stays in the valley bottom herding the deer. Occasionally a wolf will leap down in front of the running deer, causing them to stop and be attacked from the rear by the pursuing wolves. Eighty percent of the kills discovered occurred in narrow valleys. The majority of the kills were single animals killed by a pack.

In 1989, the Polish government estimated there were 913 wolves in the country. Scientists at the Polish Academy of Science put the figure between three hundred and four hundred wolves. Bobek, while saying that taking a census of animals in the wilds is very difficult, agrees with the government's estimate of close to one thousand animals. All of these guesses are in question and the lack of reliable statistics impedes decision-making.

Bobek is attempting to develop a means of estimating the number based on a feeding and metabolic study of captive wolves, which would determine food consumption of a single wolf. He says, "When the winter is over, it is very easy to find in the forest the number of red deer, roe deer, or wild boar which were killed by wolves. Knowing the daily consumption rate, you can speculate what is the population size of the wolf."

In Poland the wolf is a legally hunted game species and, according to Bobek, this has been to the wolf's benefit. "Just after the Second World War, there was a problem with wolves because they didn't have enough food inside the forest, so they were searching for domestic livestock. After the war was over our red deer population total was less than twenty thousand. In response, in the late fifties, the government started this wolf-control program. They knocked down the population from one thousand to one hundred animals. But then biologists and public opinion wanted to have more wolves," Bobek says. Unlike U.S. hunters, Polish hunters put pressure on the government saying they wanted more wolves in their hunting districts.

"Finally, the wolf obtained a good status," Bobek tells us. "He became a game species. When he was treated as a pest there was no protection. Everybody could hunt, use poison, and [do] den destruction. When the wolf became a game species, it drastically improved the status, because animals could be hunted using only guns. The government said at the beginning, 'Okay, we will wait several years. When the population level reaches a high count of animals, we will start to hunt.' The hunters accepted this, and after several years we had five hundred animals."

Bobek says that hunting is not as common in Poland as in the United States because there are more requirements that need to be fulfilled in order to become a hunter. He explains, "You must pass two exams, plus you have one year of voluntary practice. You have to participate in the hunts without hunting. After one year of such practice, you become familiar with management. Hunters are responsible for management, improving habitats, and supplemental feeding programs. They must also pay for any damages to the farmers.

"The law in Poland says that wildlife belongs to the state, even if it lives on private land, so the private person is not the owner of the wildlife. The wildlife districts are leased to the hunting clubs by the government, and the hunting clubs and the hunters are doing all the management. So they are interested very much to maintain a high level of wildlife population, because the more animals, the more they can hunt.

"They are doing tremendous voluntary work. The government controls from time to time whether the level of wildlife is managed properly. If the level is too low, they can lose the hunting district. They are taking care about everything, even the fighting of poachers, because poachers are a kind of competition. After the one year of practice, you have to pass an exam . . . and it's no problem to get a shotgun. To get a rifle, you have to hunt three years with a shotgun and pass another exam."

When presented with the possibilities of promoting the wolf as an attraction to tourists, Bugoslav readily acknowledges their value.

Earthwatch has already expressed an interest in the area where he works. Bobek, who is enthusiastic and an obvious promoter, describes it as "a kind of paradise for biology." The mountains are rich in wildlife. Besides the wolf, there are red deer, brown bear, lynx, and approximately six hundred free-ranging European bison.

One of Bugoslav's more exciting encounters in the wild was with one of the bison. "At the time they were protected animals [they became a game species in 1989] and I was looking for red deer. I don't know who—wolves or people—they chased the bison. I saw the animal charging me, and I immediately jumped into a pine. I spent about twelve hours waiting. I [had] a rifle with me, but I didn't use it."

Looking to the future, Bugoslav has bought 170 acres (68 hectares) of land in the mountains and though it isn't productive in the sense of agricultural output, he sees its value as an attractive tourist destination. He hopes in the years ahead to be able to develop it into a small entrepreneurial operation designed as a mountain resort for people wishing to see and learn more about the wolves and other wildlife of Poland. With his obvious political wisdom and a sense of entrepreneurship he should succeed.

11

Wolves of Scandinavia

WOLVES FIRST ENTERED the Scandinavian Peninsula some nine thousand years ago, migrating from the vast forest regions to the east. They existed in large numbers up until the middle of the 1800s. Then, as human settlements and animal husbandry spread, the conflict between humans and wolves escalated. This conflict coincided with a time when moose became scarce, and wolves turned to domestic livestock for food.

Today, the major Scandinavian populations of wolves exist in Finland, where the long border with Russia is also a zone of wolf migration and emigration. Historically, Finland, like Norway and Sweden, eliminated its population of wolves. Now the wolves have reestablished themselves in Finland, but the narrow neck of land that connects Finland with its Scandinavian neighbors effectively impedes wolf movement and makes them easy targets for elimination by the Lapp reindeer herders. Very few wolves survive the trip to Sweden and Norway, and if they do, they face additional hazards to survival when they get there.

Between 1850 and 1900, five thousand wolves were killed in Norway. Throughout the 1900s, their numbers continued to drop dramatically, bringing the wolf close to extirpation. We do not know if the wolf was completely eliminated and then a population reestablished by Russian wolves who crossed through Finland or if an isolated pair of wolves actually managed to survive. In the last twenty years, the number of wolves in Sweden and Norway has been estimated at around ten animals and that figure is open to debate since accurate identification and observation of the animals are difficult.

The sheep- and reindeer-herding people in these two countries maintain a strong dislike and fear of the wolf. This is clearly demonstrated by the four anti-wolf organizations in Sweden and the two in Norway. As recently as 1990, Norwegian papers carried such comments as, "Anyone entering the woods of Finnskogen should carry a gun to fight the threatening and howling wolf packs," "There will be no tourists anymore and we will not be able to enter the woods looking for berries and no more hiking in the woods," and finally, "The wolves have exterminated all the moose calves in the area."

Scandinavians have grown up with all the standard frightening fairy tales and stories about wolves killing people, but it is mostly the older rural generations that continue to believe in these myths. These are people who exert strong political and economic influence and put pressure on the government.

In Norway farmers raise 2.2 million sheep. In the northern regions, the Lapp people herd millions of reindeer. Each group believes that the wolf is a treacherous competitor. Indeed, there have been instances where wolves have killed large numbers of sheep and reindeer. In 1977, one wolf was estimated to have killed about fifty reindeer in fewer than ten days. The herders were given permission to pursue it on snowmobiles, which they did unsuccessfully for six days. They were then granted a license to shoot it from a helicopter. In a period of nineteen days the wolf was reported to have killed eighty to one hundred reindeer. One reason given for this astounding and seemingly wasteful behavior was the fact that the wolf was being pursued so intensely that it never had an opportunity to consume its kill and had to kill again every time it wanted to eat.

In the case of large sheep kills, it has been postulated that wolves become confused by the failure of sheep to take evasive action and have no stimulus to stop the killing. Whatever the reasons, farmers in both countries receive financial compensation for livestock killed by predators.

In Norway, some hundred thousand of the over 2 million sheep put out to pasture every summer do not return in the fall. Five percent are believed to be taken by predators. Of this number, two hundred are probably taken by wolves. In one year, Norway spent 23,000 kroner in predator compensation. In contrast, it was estimated that 100,000 kroner were spent in tracking down and killing one wolf that was said to be marauding near a village in southern Norway.

The story of this wolf vividly demonstrates the passionate hatred some of the people feel towards the species. The farmers of the region persuaded the government to alter a 1973 resolution designed to protect the wolf. A 2,000-kroner bounty was put on the wolf's head. As the hysteria grew, the estimated population of wolves reached eighteen animals. The suspect wolf was finally cornered and shot by Lars Saga, a hunter whose subsequent behavior seems to indicate a desire to create a folklore equal to his surname. He was photographed in his home proudly pouring champagne over the wolf's body, and he happily took it to display in the village school and in the homes of the elderly. Continuing the macabre parade, he took the body to Oslo, where members of parliament were given the opportunity to "meet" it.

Despite this sort of antagonism and pressure, wolves have continued to find places where they have bred and managed to survive, if only marginally. In particular is an area known as Finnskogen, a border district of Norway and Sweden, two hours northeast of Oslo. There have been several breedings recorded through the 1980s, and in the winter of 1990–91, three to four individuals were tracked there.

As the hysteria grew, the estimated population of wolves reached eighteen animals

The Finnskogen area is a dense forest of spruce and birch, marshy lowlands, and lakes. It is a remote wilderness, which is rare in Scandinavia. There are few inhabitants or tourists, and the main activity is timber cutting, which is done on a fairly large scale. Logging roads and frozen lakes act as travel routes for the wolves, giving researchers opportunities to track them on skis. This is also a region that has one of the densest moose (known as elk in Europe) populations in the world. Large numbers of roe deer and beaver are also part of the prey base.

While most people assume that Scandinavia would support the most wolves in Europe since there is a relatively small human population and a wild landscape, the opposite is true. The feeling of wilderness is deceptive. This is a very managed land, and the wolf is not wanted. The wildness of the wolf defies the sense of complete control that the countries seem to want. In the magazine *Hundsport,* an article in 1993 argued that hunters should be allowed to kill wolves since the wolves might kill their dogs and hunters would probably be more supportive of a species they could hunt.

Sweden and Norway had two breeding wolf packs in 1992. In Jaemtland someone tried to kill the pack with a strychnine-laced goat head. The other pack was near Vaermland, where the Swedish government denied an appeal by a pro-wolf group to spare the life of a lone female wolf who had killed a pet dog. The future of the wolf in these two countries is still in question.

Erik Isaksen

With so few wolves in Scandinavia, there has not been a great emphasis placed on studying the animals. Of the handful who have been involved in this pursuit, Erik Isaksen stands out, literally. A tall, broad-shouldered man, Erik looks like the ultimate woodsman. A thick brown beard covers most of his face, but cannot hide the wide smile that comes easily and sparkles with a touch of gold on a front tooth. His conversation is sprinkled with "yahs" and a deep chuckle that masks both his shyness of human gatherings and his strong opinions about the official scientists, or "bureaucrats" as he would describe them, who are ultimately responsible for establishing government regulations protecting the wolf.

Erik is not a university-trained scientist. Growing up in Stockholm, son of an accountant and a mother who was interested in nature, Erik spent the summers of his youth on a farm, where he remembers collecting flowers and pressing them, and looking for frogs and insects. When he was about twelve years old, his mother enrolled him in a youth organization that spent a lot of time bird watching. He also began to read Thoreau and discovered a compatriot in spirit.

With a loud bass voice, Erik booms his thoughts when he says, "I don't like society and all these consuming things. I hate it, and I've been hating it since I was about five weeks old. My mother used to say that when I was young I wanted to have a shop far away, out in the forest somewhere, where no one came to buy anything. If I had a shop, everybody would come and want to buy something and I would try to ask them, 'What do you really want this for?' and 'What do you have at home?' and 'What do your neighbors have and can't you use that instead? If you mend that you could use that instead and you don't have to buy anything.' I would make them not buy anything, because probably they don't need it. That's been my philosophy for the last twenty-five years."

When Erik finished high school, he studied photography with a man who lived in Jokkmokk (pronounced *Yukmuk*), a small village in the forest. The man had been a ranger in a national park. While learning about photography, Erik was also hiking in the mountains and learning to track. Together they found a bear, and on one occasion they tracked a wolverine to her den, where she had pups.

Hiking in the mountains, photographing, and observing wildlife were what Erik enjoyed most, and he soon discovered that the pressures of society were always going to be a problem for him. "I had a bad stomach," he says. "I get nervous and get pains in my stomach, and I have to leave and go out in the forest. That's why I didn't go to university probably." Because of this combination of mental and physical discomfort with modern society, Erik decided to go to Greenland for photography, wildlife, and "the simple life."

He says, "I wanted to see the people. I went there one summer, traveled on my own, met a lot of people. If you're the sort of people who come and are open to them, it's easy to make friendships. I wanted to get to know the people, too—the way of living. All the time I am going alone. If you go with friends you keep together and talk about Sweden."

Erik lived with a family, helped out with any chores that needed to be done, and contributed money when he could. After a time he felt as though he was part of the family. When they went hunting, he went with them.

"When young boys grow up and go hunting with the older people to learn, you never get any cash yourself because it's the older man who shoots all the time and you just help. You get your share of meat, for your dogs, but you don't get any cash. That's why it's hard for the young people to get into it, because they want cash to buy a new radio or tape recorder. So they'd rather go work in the shop where they get paid. If they go with the old hunter, they always get meat and food and everything they need."

In this culture Erik found people who matched his own philosophy of living. He explains, "With the Eskimos, that's where I learned how to do it [mend things]. I mean you go and look around. They don't have much cash and that's a way of living. They don't go to the North Pole because that's rather stupid, but they go hunting in the same environment and they look like gypsies. Most of the things they have is from the rubbish dump. They borrow from their neighbors. If you don't need your car, then I borrow it. It's better that someone uses it until you need it, and then you say, 'I might need my car,' so I give it back to you. It's this way of sharing that they used to have."

Erik's father was a hunter, but he himself had never hunted until he went to live with the Greenlanders. "I shot some birds and seals. I'm not interested in trophy hunting. I'm happy if they get a walrus, then we have food." The diet of the Greenlanders would be a shock to most urban people, but Erik found it easy to adjust to. As he tells us, "You go into a supermarket and everything is in small boxes and you don't know what's in it, some premade thing. You are used to mostly eating that food, unnatural food. In Sweden, old people, eighty years old, born on a poor farm, slaughtered their own animals and fished, and so blood and using the brain is not that special to them. They are interested in what the Eskimos eat, but it's easy to find people who just go, 'Can you eat that?' and they never know what their grandparents did." Erik has eaten seal blubber, fresh, warm liver, flippers, stomach contents, kidney, muscle, and brain. He has eaten meat raw, boiled, dried, and aged until it's slightly green, which is often the color of the person listening to him recount his culinary experiences.

While Erik learned much about the wildlife in Greenland, he didn't learn much more about tracking. As he says, "You mostly hunt around the sea, for seals and walrus, and there's no tracking involved. We don't walk on land. It's on the ice all the time. You learn how to take care of yourself."

In 1976 when Erik returned to Sweden, he moved to Jokkmokk and reestablished contact with the man who had introduced him to tracking. He was now employed by the government in a tracking program and so Erik got involved. As he explains, "You can't get

someone to work on wolf study so easy . . . these people have jobs."
The majority of wolf work is not funded or underfunded and there is
no money for research assistants. Erik's primary responsibility is
tracking and working as a field technician. This has included a study
of lynx, a five-year summer survey of otters, and a study of gray seals
in the Baltic, both of which have been affected by PCBs. Funding for
his work has come from the Natural History Museum in Stockholm
and from the World Wildlife Fund.

In the late 1970s, reports of wolves began to increase. "People
started seeing wolves everywhere," he says. "If you just sit in your
office in Stockholm you start getting all these reports. People phone
you, and you get letters and . . . newspaper articles about people seeing
wolves. . . . You would think there are some fifty wolves in Sweden. If
you send someone out to check, lots of them are lynx and foxes. . . .
That's mainly why we have so few wolves, because we check them.
If we didn't check them we would have more wolves. If we say they
have six or seven, then the local people, they have twenty. The game
warden, he has to be diplomatic, so he has somewhere between. He
has twelve. So it depends on who you ask."

Since 1978 Erik has worked on the wolf study in one way or another.
Winter tracking has been the main method of gathering information.
Some Scandinavian scientists would like to begin trapping and radio
collaring the wolves, but the cost could be very high, both fiscally
and for the wolf population.

Erik explains this conundrum. "If you start catching them it costs
money. A few will die and you hurt them. If you only have this one
pack, . . . if some die by accident, it's bad—bad propaganda. That's
one of the problems, because they're so few. In Sweden fox traps
have been banned for a long time. If you start to trap [wolves] and
radio collar them in an area, and people don't like them, it's hard to
work. If it's not a wilderness area, you aren't alone and people will
see what you're doing. If you catch them, people will say, 'But why
don't you take them to Stockholm, where you want them? When you
have them in your hands, why don't you put them somewhere?' I
don't think it would be very wise to do a study like this when the
local people oppose it."

For the time being, tracking remains the main means of research,
and Erik Isaksen has the most experience in this area. It is a time-

consuming, labor-intensive process. Erik is especially concerned that he not disturb the wolf in whatever it might be doing. He tells us, "I try not to see them. If they are in an area, if I find fresh tracks, then I make a circle some twenty kilometers [12 mi] around. If it looks like the wolf is in this circle, I'll go tracking his old trail. Then the next day, I'll go around again. If the wolf is still there, I'll go track old trails—if I know about any. When the wolf goes out of the circle, I'll make a new circle to find where it stopped. If I decide it's left this area, I'll go in and track it to see what it's been doing. There's always a moose carcass or several carcasses in the area, and I try to see how it chased it and how it hunted. We follow these tracks to see mainly where there are wolves and how many, if they have pups or are single animals."

Determining how many wolves there are, or even if they are wolves, is very difficult. There may be a stray dog in the area or a lynx that has spread its claws for better balance on the snow's crust, or the wolves may be walking in one another's footsteps.

Erik laughs as he tells us, "My field notes are a mess. When you go tracking them, there are so many interpretations. You don't know what is imagination. That makes it fun in a way, but it makes it very hard to use the data. I describe where the tracks are on the map. I see if it's a pack or single animals, what sex it is [based on] how they urinate or blood from the female in estrous. Maybe there will be a litter. At the kills, I try to sketch the chase, what parts are eaten, and when it was killed. Sometimes we take the bones for the marrow, and sometimes the whole animal. If you take the carcass away though, then they have to go kill more. Often we leave them and let them eat what they want."

The wolves are mostly hunting moose, but so are the humans. As Erik explains, this is part of the problem. "In Sweden, we harvest 130,000 moose a year. So if a hunter finds a few moose that are killed by wolves, they think it is a waste of meat. Every moose is supposed to end up in a freezer. That's how they're supposed to die in Sweden." According to Erik, the wolves do take a lot of moose and he claims they're smarter than the wolves in Minnesota. He tells of wolves killing cows and calves single-handedly. The bones he has examined have had good marrow content, so they appear to be healthy animals. However, without other means of analyzing the remains, it is difficult to know whether the animals were sick or weakened in other ways.

Erik continues to use photography in his work. Some of his most dramatic pictures capture the playful interaction between a wolf and a domestic dog. The wolves tend to be shy of humans when moving, but when they stop in area they seem to lose some of their fear. They also seem to be attracted to dogs, and Erik has documented little aggression. The wolf Erik photographed in June of 1989 was eventually chased away with rubber bullets. It moved on, but shortly thereafter was illegally killed.

Erik published his photos of this wolf-dog interaction in a Norwegian publication, and though he doesn't have a university degree, he has published articles about his work and findings. Looking back on his career and choices of lifestyle, Erik doesn't express many regrets. "If I had this education, I might end up as a bureaucrat. Now, there is no chance of that. They know what I can do, so there are no formalities. I never tried to apply for a job. I don't have a résumé. If I had the degree, and I had projects I could do myself, it would be more fun in a way, but most people end up sitting in an office, hiring people. I couldn't do that because of problems with my stomach. I would have to be another person."

Erkki Pulliainen

The wolfman of Finland, founder of the Green Party, a wolf expert, a professor, and an elected politician, Erkki Pulliainen has researched wolves longer than anyone and in doing so has become one of the most recognizable figures in Finland. He has written ten books— three on wolves, one on dogs, and the rest on other wildlife. One story that I can neither confirm nor refute describes the wolfman's visit to a zoo. To prove that wolves are not bloodthirsty animals, he covered himself with blood and went unprotected into the wolf pen. The wolves were intimidated by the strange sight and smell and kept away.

Erkki is driven, colorful, and opinionated. "[In parliament] you should have an opinion of everything you have in front of you. Absolutely. You know that when the first Green movement (it was called ecological movement) arose in France, it did make a very big mistake. It said, 'The only thing is protection of nature and environments. We do not have any political opinions on the other things, on social aspects, and so on. We totally deny the significance of foreign policy.' It was an extremely bad mistake. It is absolutely important that we have in the order of importance, at the hierarchy, the environmental questions and nature protection questions, but at the same time, we must have a solution to every social and budget thing which is in front of us in decision making."

In 1961, Erkki was a young unemployed muckster who happened to be attending college at the same time that wolves were expanding their range from Russia to Finland. His father had moved to St. Petersburg as a child and eventually became a successful businessman and director of a shoe factory. Then the Revolution came, and he journeyed to Finland via the woods of Karelia, just as the wolves are doing now. In Finland the elder Pulliainen hid in a cellar for one year to avoid the Soviet death sentence. He next moved to Germany, where he became the head of another shoe factory. This odyssey continued to many countries and finally back to Finland, where he married at the age of fifty.

Erkki is the oldest son of that marriage. His brother and two sisters continued in the business, while Erkki sought his path in nature. As a small boy he wandered the woods collecting nests, butterflies, and beetles. He started at the university in 1958, avoided the army because of a disability, and graduated in two years, a rate that Erkki tells today's students is too fast. He had a degree, but no prospects. His youth and inexperience worked against him. He says now, "You must live it, not only read and come from examinations."

While he was taking the fast track through university, the Finnish people were extirpating the wolf, just as the Norwegian and Swedish people had been doing. The wolves began to come in from Karelia and the long, shared border with Russia. His research now shows that approximately fifty-five wolves came into Finland in 1959 and every single one was killed, a fact he confirms because he has studied their carcasses.

In 1961, while Erkki was working on his doctorate, a professor announced in class that the Finnish Foundation wanted to finance a study on the wolves of northern Karelia. Erkki replied, "I am interested in anything that pays money." From that exchange, thirty years of wolf research was born.

As is usually the case, the research would have been more efficient if it had begun earlier. In the two years between wolf immigration and wolf research, Finland and Karelia went to war, not against each other, but against the wolf. There were five hundred soldiers in the field with the express purpose of killing wolves. Cars lined roadsides, and hundreds of men took up arms throughout the countryside. Erkki's first studies were done using three years of newspaper reports. He estimates that he read ten thousand newspapers on microfiche. He then had the job of organizing the research on living wolves.

Finland is 660 miles (1,062 km) from north to south and has an area of 130,000 square miles (338,000 km^2) with a population of fifty to seventy-five wolves. In the reindeer husbandry area, wolves are unprotected and shot on sight. In addition, communities along the eastern border can kill any wolves they see.

Erkki took a creative approach to his wolf research. In 1967, he approached the commander of the nation's border guards. There were 1,500 in the field each day, patrolling this isolated line. Why not give the guards something else to look for? They could do a daily wolf, bear, wolverine, and lynx track survey. The commander agreed and for twenty years the patrol has recorded every crossing by single wolf or pack. Now Erkki has an indelible picture of wolf movements back and forth across this frontier.

He describes the situation. "Wolves may cross the frontier every day. It's very difficult to say how many wolves we do have. It may be a moment when all the wolves inhabiting the frontier area are on the Russian side of the border and there is nobody on the Finnish side. Then the amount may be ten to twenty, and the next day it may be more than fifty, and we have received an immigration of wolves from the east."

In the gap between the '61 study and '67 border strategy, Erkki raised twenty-one wolves in captivity and set up a research station in Lapland. His years of work have given him many memories. He reminisces about a few. "Once I thought some meat was on the ice of a lake. You know, something a poacher had left. He had dropped the meat of a moose. I think that a wolf was very hungry but did not touch the frozen meat. I wondered why. And then I recognized that the trapper had dropped his box of tobacco near the meat, and the wolf was scared of the smell and left the meat.

"We have received young wolves who stop and are so scared of a ski track of a human that they do not cross it, and we have urban wolves which would walk along the highways, across the highways, through the yards of houses, through the yards of factories, and everywhere. . . . In order to survive you have to be familiar with urban conditions and their rules . . . to detect what is dangerous and what is not dangerous. Urban wolves take risks a wilderness wolf would never take," Erkki tells us.

"Once I have been in a very serious situation in the field work. My hands were frozen. It was near a reindeer fence in eastern Lapland. The temperature was minus forty-five degrees Celsius [-49° Fahrenheit] and I drove a snow scooter. Suddenly, I wondered why my fingers were not moving. Then I stopped at the reindeer fence and beat on a pine tree. The nerves begin to move inside the hands very slowly, and very slowly they begin to warm. I asked our doctor what happened. He said that was a very dangerous situation, only some minutes more and he'd have had to amputate both hands. That is the most serious situation in the field work during these years. Otherwise I have been very lucky."

Urban wolves take risks a wilderness wolf would never take

Erkki has noted that eskers—long gravel ridges left behind by glaciers—are favorite travel routes for wolves. He has also seen that wolves do not detect the danger of cars. They have lost as many as ten wolves in a year to collisions.

Erkki is a public figure and recognizes the need to forsake his field experiences for the political arena. He says, "I have been in city council previously. Now I'm in parliament. No election campaign, nothing at all. In city council election I have second highest number of votes. No advertising, no campaign, nothing at all. If newspaper reporter asks, I have always said, I'm available if you want, but otherwise I have other things to do."

Erkki Pullainen says in defense of his career, "If I as a human being have a small chance to influence decision-making and save some nature for future generations, why should I not leave my own desires, primary desires, and do it to participate in decision-making, in speaking in parliament? Since I know a little bit about ecology, I know a little bit about environment and protection and so on, and it might be that in my position at the parliament there would not be a person who happens to know so much as I do. If another man's decisions had destroyed all my animals, all my habitats, what is there to study if everything has been lost?"

Erkki's move into politics is a natural outgrowth of his work on wolves. The wolf is more than a canid, it is a high-order predator, a symbol of the food pyramid and ecology of the world. In protecting the wolf, we have to protect the habitat, the prey, the total environment. The Green Party is established to put an ecological perspective on political and social decisions, and it is fitting that an animal that brings with it so much controversy and has such a strong social instinct should be a symbol for ecological sanity.

Postscript

THE WOLF HAS ATTRACTED a wide assortment of personalities to its cause. The supporters, the researchers, and the curious cross the spectrum of society. If we can learn from the researchers as well as the research, the lesson would reflect the complexity of the organism. We find people studying the wolf with a passion that is seldom seen in wildlife fields. Jane Goodall's chimpanzees and the work on the mountain gorilla are the only comparable efforts. Like the wolf, these primates elicit great public interest and support, plus a legion of individuals who work as volunteers and researchers to complete their story.

While the wolf has been pushed almost to the brink of extinction, the work of researchers and a vigilant public has helped them to regain a strong and expanding base. Wolf research focuses on hybridization where wolves and dogs intermix in locations crowded with human development; on predation where wolf populations live among livestock; on the mechanics of wolf immigration, extirpation, and reintroduction in frontier areas of expansion; and on the society and function of the pack when they are removed from the everyday influences of an expanding human population.

The questions we wrestle with are related to reintroduction, how to change public misconceptions, how to replace displaced prey species, and how to fit a wild animal into a managed system. The International Union of Conservation of Nature's Wolf Specialist Group now wrestles with global questions, and a new European organization (the European Wolf Network) coordinates the data from that continent's many diverse countries.

We think of the Scandinavian countries as the portion of Europe where wilderness has its greatest foothold, yet that is the area where the wolves have their greatest struggle for acceptance. In a war-torn Middle East, researchers have still found the drive to study the wolf.

In the end, it seems as though the researcher—a profession that often attracts people more comfortable with wildlife than humans—

often turns educator or politician. Weaver, Carrera, Isaksen, and Theberge cry out for understanding and acceptance; Mech devotes his energies to establishing an International Wolf Center; and Fonseca organizes a citizen group. Meanwhile, Bobek, Ream, and Pulliainen turn to politics to influence their parts of the world.

We still have to answer the questions of genetics, introduced diseases, human expansion, and natural cycles. We will have more Isle Royales to surprise us when we think that we have everything figured out. While there are ethical questions to raise about some research methods, there is no end to the questions research can ask.

What does seem clear in the maze of government policy, anguished political and cultural debate, and exploding technology is an image of wolves that is far from the slavering beasts of the past. Through our research and education we are returning to the American Indian image of the wolf as provider and protector. When we accept the wolf as an integral part of the natural world, perhaps we can also remove the hatreds and behaviors in human society that we have tried to assign to the wolf of myth.

A Timeline of Wolf History

1791 William Bartram describes red wolf

1813 Last wolf shot in Denmark

1835 Last wolf in Netherlands

1838 Michigan puts bounty on wolf

1870 Wolves extirpated in New Brunswick, Prince Edward Island, and Nova Scotia

1872 Yellowstone National Park established

1880 Yellowstone superintendent Philetus Norris's annual report notes that nearly all Yellowstone wolves were extirpated

1893 New Mexico–Arizona Territory passes Bounty Act allowing counties to raise money to pay bounty hunters for dead wolves

1909 New Mexico Territory provides $15 bounties

1911 Wolves extinct in Newfoundland

1914 Ranchers pressure Congress to enact legislation to involve U.S. Biological Survey in conducting predator control experiments

1915 Superintendent of Yellowstone National Park renews wolf extermination campaign. Federal law provides for extermination on federal lands

1921 Michigan reviews bounty

1925 Michigan reinstates bounty

1927 Polish wildlife law declared the wolf a game species and a pest

1931 Wolf research by Sigurd Olson begins in Superior National Forest, Minnesota. In this decade wolves recolonize Riding Mountain National Park in Manitoba

1933 Aldo Leopold publishes *Game Management*

1938 Sigurd Olson wolf thesis published

1939 Adolph Murie begins research in Mount McKinley (Denali) National Park

1940 Isle Royale, in Lake Superior off the Minnesota shore, becomes a national park.

1941 Murie concludes field work. Federal program for extermination of wolves on federal land terminated (24,132 killed since 1915)

1944 Adolph Murie publishes *The Wolves of Mount McKinley*. Aldo Leopold writes the essay "Thinking Like a Mountain," published in *A Sand County Almanac*

1946 62,600 wolves killed in USSR (one-year total)

1947 Ian McTaggert Cowan does pioneering research in Canada

1948 Milt Stenlund begins research in Superior National Forest

1949 Air ban in Superior National Forest prevents shooting from planes. First wolf tracks found on Isle Royale. Elk reach overpopulation levels in Riding Mountain National Park, despite presence of wolf

1950 Polish wolf population estimated at 1,000

1953 Conclusion of Milt Stenlund's study in Superior National Forest

1954 Wolves legally protected in Israel

1955 Ian McTaggert Cowan publishes British Columbia study

1956 Thirty wolves bountied in Michigan

1957 Seven wolves bountied in Michigan

1958 Durward Allen begins Isle Royale project, with L. David Mech as researcher. Doug Pimlott starts wolf study in Algonquin Park, Ontario. Richard Dorer of the Minnesota Conservation Department decides to end wolf control by game personnel on wilderness portions of Superior National Forest. Milt Stenlund's thesis published

1959 One wolf bountied in Michigan

1960 Bounty ended in Michigan

1961 Large expansion of Russian wolves into Finland. Completion of Mech study on Isle Royale wolves. Erkki Pulliainen begins work on Finnish wolves

1962 L. David Mech completes thesis on Isle Royale wolves

1964 Doug Pimlott and Paul Joslin begin two-year survey of remaining red wolves (result: wolves found only in Upper

Texas Gulf Coast and Louisiana)

1965 Doug Pimlott completes Algonquin Park study. Minnesota governor Karl Rolvaag refuses to sign bill appropriating money to bounties, effectively ending bounty hunting that began nine years before statehood. Michigan gives legal protection to wolves. Minnesota makes bounties illegal. Wolf listed as endangered in Sweden

1966 Dave Mech begins part-time work in Minnesota's Superior National Forest. Endangered Species Act 89–669. Publication of *Wolves of Isle Royale*

1967 First Wolf Symposium held in Maryland. Red wolf declared endangered species

1968 Dave Mech and Dan Frenzel begin Minnesota studies

1969 U.S. Fish and Wildlife Service with U.S. Forest Service and State of Minnesota establish Minnesota research program and hire Dave Mech. Minnesota passes bill for Directed Predator Control

1970s Last native wolves eliminated in Finland

1970 Publication of *The Wolf: Ecology and Behavior of an Endangered Species* by L. David Mech. Full-time research by Mech in Superior National Forest. First timber wolf sanctuary in Minnesota established in Superior National Forest. Wolf given protection in Spain

1971 Wolf made a big-game species in part of Spain

1972 Shooting wolves from air made illegal in Alaska

1973 Wolf fully protected by Endangered Species Act. First evidence of timber wolves in Wisconsin since extirpation. Census in Italy counts one hundred wolves. Wolf protected in Norway (none left). Poland bans the use of poison for wolf control

1974 Polish wolf population estimated at 100. Luigi Boitani and Erik Zimen begin Italian study with Mech's help. L. David Mech, Bill Robinson, Tom Weise, and students work on Michigan wolf transplant. Minnesota prohibits public from killing wolves in any manner. Spanish census: 1,400

1975 Vic Van Ballenberghe, A. W. Erickson, and D. Byman publish Lake Superior Shore study. Lu Carbyn begins radio tracking study in Canada at Riding Mountain National Park.

Rolf Peterson takes over Isle Royale study. Jan van Haaften proposes research in Portugal. Poland restored game status for wolf. Approximate beginning of natural recolonization in Wisconsin

1977 Large expansion of Russian wolves into Finland. Roy McBride hired to assess Mexican wolf population

1978 Eastern Timber Wolf Recovery Team Plan is produced. Timber wolf reclassified from endangered to threatened in Minnesota. Red wolves released on Bull's Island, South Carolina. Wolves recolonize western Glacier National Park, Montana

1979 Twenty-five wolves in Wisconsin (all in Douglas County, except for one pack near the city of Wausau). Mexican Wolf Recovery Team appointed to advise Fish and Wildlife Service. Last red wolves from wilds brought to Tacoma, Washington

1980 On Isle Royale, fifty wolves and five packs. Red wolf declared biologically extinct in the wild. Spain prohibits use of poison for predators

1982 Roy McBride estimates Mexican wolf population at "no more than fifty breeding pairs." Mexican Wolf Recovery Plan filed in Federal Court. Isle Royale has fourteen wolves. Jan van Haaften research in Portugal

1983 First systematic study of wolves in the Yukon. U.S. Fish and Wildlife Service proposes shared wolf management with Minnesota Department of Natural Resources. A consortium of fifteen environmental groups contest the plan and win in court

1984 Large expansion of Russian wolves into Finland

1985 Wolf-Dall sheep study in Kluane area of Yukon. Completion of public-attitude study in Minnesota by Steven Kellert

1986 Study of wolf distribution and wolf-prey relationships in Yukon. Polish wolf population estimated at 888. Four pairs of red wolves taken to Alligator River National Wildlife Refuge, North Carolina. Study of wolf ecology in Denali National Park, Alaska, begun. Wolf Fund begun (for reintroduction of wolves into Yellowstone National Park)

1987 First red wolf litter born in wilds at Alligator River National

Wildlife Refuge. U.S. Fish and Wildlife approval of Northern Rocky Mountain Wolf Recovery Plan

1988 Live trapping of wolves on Isle Royale (by Rolf Peterson). Four adult red wolves die in Alligator River. One adult female red wolf dies on Bull's Island, South Carolina. July 8, four red wolves released on Bull's Island. Yellowstone fires. International Wolf Center site reaffirmed for Ely, Minnesota. Study of caribou, elk, and wolf in Jasper National Park, Alberta. Portugal gives wolves full legal protection (population estimate: 150–200). Youth in Great Britain (9–15) rate wolves among most disliked animals. Recommendation to reintroduce wolves in Yellowstone National Park. Spain's wolf population estimated at one thousand

1989 Plans for breeding Mexican wolves at three sites. Isle Royale's population winter inventory: eleven. Wisconsin's population: twenty-eight. Three municipalities in Quebec vote to place bounties on wolves. The Fish and Game Association (private organization) announces bounties for wolf

1991 Preliminary survey of wolves conducted in Saudi Arabia

1993 Finnish parliament gives the wolf game animal status. European Federation for the Wolf (EFW) forms in Leige, Belgium. Researchers confirm that wolves had crossed the Alps into France and are in the Mercantour Nature Reserve above Nice. Yellowstone Planning Program Report and public review. U.S. Fish and Wildlife Service announced that animal shot near Yellowstone in the fall of 1992 is a purebred wolf. International Wolf Center opens in Ely, Minnesota

Index

About the Authors

Mike Link and Kate Crowley draw upon a wide range of experiences for their writings. Mike, director of the Northwoods Audubon Center, has an enthusiasm for adventures as diverse as paddling a wild river or teaching at Northland College and the National Audubon Society. Mike is the author of three books and many magazine and newspaper articles, along with seven Voyageur Press books co-written with his wife Kate Crowley. Mike spends time in numerous outdoor pursuits with Kate, who shares his love of the outdoors. Mike's daughter Julie is studying Natural Resources at the University of Minnesota. His son Matt died in a kayak accident while teaching in New Zealand. It is in his memory that Mike and Kate's latest book is dedicated.

Kate Crowley, a naturalist and writer, supervised the monorail interpretive program at the Minnesota Zoo for six years and contributed articles to zoo publications. In addition, she has volunteered for the Minnesota Valley National Wildlife Refuge and served for more than five years on the board of the Minnesota Naturalist Association. Kate's two children, Alyssa and Jonathon, are completing college studies in Wyoming and Minnesota.